Mary Berry is well known as the author of more than seventy cookery books with total sales of over 5 million. She has presented a number of television series and is currently a judge on *The Great British Bake Off*. She contributes to radio programmes and cookery magazines, and is loved for her practical and unfussy approach to preparing and serving food. She gives many demonstrations around the country but when she is at home, she loves to be with her family and tending to her garden – her other great passion.

Mary Berry's
Family Sunday Lunches

Over 150 delicious recipes for a relaxed Sunday lunch

headline

Photo captions

Page 29 Tom (Mary's son)

Page 41 (from left to right) Sarah (Mary's daughter-in-law), Paul (Mary's husband), Tom, Mary, Hobie (Mary's grandson) and Annabel (Mary's daughter)

Page 99 Hobie

Page 142 Paul

Page 182 Lucy Young (Mary's assistant and friend)

Copyright © 2011 Mary Berry

Photographs © William Shaw
Photo on page 182 © Juliet Piddington

First published in 2011 by
HEADLINE PUBLISHING GROUP

1

Cataloguing in Publication Data is available from the British Library

ISBN 978 0 7553 6090 1

Photographs by William Shaw
Designed by Nick Venables
Edited by Jo Roberts-Miller
Typeset in Minion by Nick Venables
Printed and bound in the UK by Butler Tanner and Dennis Ltd, Frome

HEADLINE PUBLISHING GROUP
An Hachette UK Company
338 Euston Road, London NW1 3BH

www.headline.co.uk
www.hachette.co.uk

Contents

Introduction

My first book on Sunday lunches was published in 1982 and, then, they were a very traditional affair – usually just roasts and a traditional pudding. Now, though, Sunday lunch is much more informal – still the occasional roast but, more often than not, a one-pot dish and always a great way of having friends and family round.

When I was asked to write this book, it was suggested that I update the original but I found as I went back to the old book that it needed more than an update. I decided I'd like to start from scratch and use the recipes I make for my own family and friends as a kick-off point. Nearly all of these recipes are far simpler to make and far quicker to assemble than their older counterparts, and yet they still bring wonderful results. More and more of us have electric mixers, blenders and processors, which cut out a lot of the hard work, and every recipe has tips on how to prepare the dish in advance and whether it freezes or not, which lets you get one step ahead.

So much has changed in the last 30 years – not only have Sundays become less formal but we have a far greater choice of ingredients. All those years ago, the vegetable selection was quite limited – you didn't grow or find fennel and butternut squash, they were almost unknown. We have become much more adventurous with our herbs, too – no need to use dried as fresh are readily available and far better; and what a choice there is now in the dairy department – from crème fraîche to mascarpone, ricotta and feta. All these new ingredients have transformed our recipes, making old favourites into new favourites and giving Sunday lunch classics a real twist. Nowadays, it is easy enough to buy most of the sauce accompaniments in the shop but we always try to make our own – the recipes really are so quick to do and taste better.

My husband Paul's eyes always light up when it's Sunday lunch – it means the young or friends are coming and there's bound to be a pudding! Puddings are out for us in the week but Sunday lunch wouldn't be the same without one, so I've included a large number of cold desserts and hot puddings to choose from. If there's time and our children and grandchildren are around we tend to make a crumble using fruit in season (try the *Quick orange and plum crumble* on page 209) but if I'm short of time I'll chose a cold pudding made well ahead, like *Wicked chocolate mousse* (see page 197) or *Early pink rhubarb brûlée* (see page 192). Most of the dessert recipes can be made well in advance, so there's no excuse not to have one on a Sunday. The *Late summer pudding* (see page 199) is best made the day before and all the pies can be frozen cooked, so they need only be thawed, brought back to room temperature and then reheated for about fifteen minutes. If you have meringues in the cupboard or homemade ice cream in the freezer, you're only ever a few easy steps away from serving a delicious treat.

In the past, family lunches were always here at home but, now that the young have spread their wings, they often host it themselves. They'll follow many of these family recipes, often with the addition of home-grown vegetables. Our daughter, Annabel, is a great one for salads and she grows hers in neat lines in knee-high troughs at her back door. It's amazing what she's managed to produce – baby carrots, dwarf beans, numerous salad leaves and tomatoes. Son, Thomas, grows his in raised beds, which he is immensely proud of. In fact, his girls tell me that, when he gets home from work in the summer, the raised beds are his first port of call to check on how things are going; Sarah, our daughter in law, is a great one for cooking vegetables ahead. Tom's twins, Abby and Grace, will very often help in the kitchen or even make the pudding when they are staying with me – ice creams and meringues are the favourite with them – lots of bowls to lick! Annabel's boys, four-year-old Hobie and six-year-old Louis, have a penchant for chopping up – both are good with knives but have to be carefully watched and are really very useful when we're making a casserole with vegetables.

The joy with more relaxed Sunday lunches is that, even if you are exceedingly busy, you can do the prepare-ahead dishes, such as *Braised lamb shanks with apple and caper sauce* (see page 62) and *Pheasant casserole with thyme and prunes* (see page 95) in the winter, or *Chilled garlic chicken breasts with tomato salad* (see page 176) and *Cold poached salmon with avocado and pickled ginger* (see page 179) in the summer. I have a special way of cooking vegetables ahead to perfection and then reheating them in a hot oven (see page 131) and roast potatoes cooked ahead may sound awful but, take it from me, they are fantastic! I always think that green and seasonal veg are best cooked at the last moment, though. At a push and for a crowd, you can cook the veg ahead quickly and then plunge them into cold water to stop the cooking. This is what the chefs do. But if it's veg from the garden, I'll pick it in the morning and then cook it when I need it.

If I'm cooking for numbers on a Sunday, I often do a curry, hence the Winter Curry chapter. At New Year, we had thirty-five for lunch and we cooked all the curry recipes included here and they went down a treat! There's something for everyone and, although I have made them fairly mild, if you want them hot, you can spice them up. The huge advantage of curries is that most of them can be made ahead and frozen, so you have time to set everything out, lay the table and greet your guests, safe in the knowledge that the food is all ready. A word of advice – you'll always need more mango chutney than you think! And look out for mini poppadoms in the shops – they were a hit when we served them.

I so hope you will enjoy my choice of recipes – don't overwork yourself! Sunday lunch is all about being at home with family or friends; having a relaxed, delicious lunch followed by a seasonal walk.

Mary Berry
www.maryberry.co.uk

Acknowledgements

Firstly it is Lucy Young who I thank more than I can say. Luc has worked by my side for 21 years and is responsible for my working life and everything that goes into books; we jointly plan the testing of recipes and deciding what goes in the book right through to working with the publishers. Lucinda, who is wonderful and has worked with us for 10 years, tests the recipes with us – testing and re-testing until they are perfect and at their very best. Izzie Forrest has, as usual, had a great input in the game section.

Jo Roberts-Miller at Headline has been working on this book from the beginning and is a joy to work with, making sure every copy is perfect and the book is just right, keeping us on schedule. William Shaw has taken stunning photographs and Vicky Smallwood has produced beautiful food for the photo shoot – huge thank you to you both.

Felicity Bryan has been my book agent for donkey's years and is always there for advice, along with Michele and their wonderful team.

Finally, thank you to Paul my husband and our family and, of course, you the readers for still supporting me and helping me love my work.

Canapés

Tiny roasted veg and goat's cheese parcels

MAKES 40

1 small aubergine, cut into 1cm (½ in) dice

1 red pepper, cut into 1cm (½ in) dice

1 medium courgette, cut into 1cm (½ in) dice

½ medium onion, chopped finely

2 tbsp olive oil

100g (4 oz) firm goat's cheese, cut into 1cm (½ in) dice

3 tbsp fresh basil, roughly chopped

10 x filo pastry sheets (25 x 22cm/10 x 8½ in)

melted butter, to assemble

To prepare ahead
Can be made up to a day ahead – reheated in a hot oven until piping hot or cooked to serve. Freezes well uncooked.

To cook in the Aga
Roast the vegetables on the floor of the roasting oven for 30 minutes. Cook the parcels on the floor of the roasting oven for about 12 minutes.

Serve these warm for any special occasion. It is a good idea to chill the block of goats' cheese in the freezer for about 15 minutes to make it easier to cut.

Preheat the oven to 200°C/Fan 180°C/Gas 6.

Measure all the chopped vegetables into a roasting tin. Drizzle with the oil and season with salt and pepper. Roast in the preheated oven for 25–30 minutes, or until soft and tinged brown. Set aside to cool.

Mix the goat's cheese and basil into the cold vegetables.

Brush one sheet of filo with melted butter. Cut the sheet into four long strips. Spoon a teaspoon of the mixture on to one end and fold in alternating directions to make a triangle. Brush the top with a little melted butter and place on a baking sheet. Continue with the remainder of the filo sheets and filling.

Bake in the preheated oven for 12–15 minutes until golden and crisp.

Sun-blushed tomato and quail's egg tartlets

MAKES 24

6 quail's eggs

4 tbsp mayonnaise

24 sun-blushed tomatoes, skin removed

celery salt, for seasoning

24 parsley leaves

Pastry

75g (3 oz) plain flour

40g (1½ oz) cold butter

25g (1 oz) Parmesan cheese, grated

1 tsp Marmite

2 tbsp water

To prepare ahead
The tartlet cases can be made up to 2 days ahead and filled up to 4 hours ahead. The empty cases freeze well.

To cook in the Aga
Bake the pastry on the grid shelf on the floor of the roasting oven for about 10–12 minutes.

These look so lovely and the Marmite in the pastry gives them a lovely colour and savoury taste. As a variation, replace the quail's egg with crumbled feta cheese. Sun-blushed tomatoes are available from the deli section in your supermarket and are sometimes called sun-ripened tomatoes.

You will need a 24-hole mini muffin tin.

To make the pastry, measure the flour and butter into a processor and whiz until it looks like breadcrumbs. Add the cheese, Marmite and water and whiz again until it forms a ball. Roll the pastry out very thinly on a floured surface and stamp into 24 rounds using a 5cm (2 in) cutter. Line the mini muffin tin with the pastry and prick each base. Chill for 30 minutes.

Preheat the oven to 180°C/Fan 160°C/Gas 4.

Bake the pastry blind in the preheated oven for 12–15 minutes until golden and cooked through. Set aside to cool for a few minutes and then carefully remove and cool on a wire rack.

Boil the quail's eggs for 3 minutes until cooked. Peel and cut each one into quarters.

Spoon half a teaspoon of mayonnaise into the base of each cold tartlet case. Top with a sun-blushed tomato and arrange a quarter quail's egg on top of this. Sprinkle with a little pepper and celery salt and garnish with a parsley leaf.

Serve cold – these look stunning served on a black plate or a piece of slate.

Triple prawns with horseradish dip

MAKES ABOUT 40

500g (1 lb 2 oz) shelled North
    Atlantic cooked prawns
a few sprigs of dill or parsley,
    to garnish

Tomato and horseradish dip

3 tbsp mayonnaise

3 tbsp tomato ketchup

3 tbsp crème fraîche

1 tbsp lemon juice

2 tbsp creamed horseradish

1 tsp Worcestershire sauce

a dash of caster sugar

To prepare ahead
The sauce can be made up
to 2 days ahead. The prawns
can be threaded on to their
skewers up to a day ahead.
Not suitable for freezing.

Recently we had a crowd over for a summer Sunday lunch and, rather than serve a first course, I did three bites to go with Pimm's. The favourite were these prawns. I used bamboo party skewers – I bought mine in Sainsbury's but they are also available online. Being frugal I put them to wash in the cutlery basket of the dishwasher and they came out a treat!

You will need 40 bamboo skewers or cocktail sticks.

To make the dip, mix all the ingredients together and season with salt and pepper. Depending on your taste, you may like to add a little more lemon juice or caster sugar. Spoon into a small, shallow bowl.

Push three prawns on to each skewer and arrange the skewers on one side of a large flat dish with the bowl of dip on the other side. If the bowl is inclined to slip, fix it to the flat dish with Blu-Tack.

Garnish the plate with sprigs of dill or parsley. Hand them round and have a separate bowl for discarded skewers.

Smoked angels on horseback

MAKES 9 CANAPÉS

1 x 85g can smoked oysters

3–4 rashers thin streaky unsmoked bacon

To prepare ahead
Can be prepared up to a day ahead and cooked as detailed (right) to serve. Not suitable for freezing.

To cook in the Aga
Roast on the floor of the roasting oven for about 8 minutes.

Canned oysters are a great ingredient to use as you can keep them on the shelf until you need them. Of course, they are quite different from fresh oysters, which have to be really fresh and are a chore to open. There are usually nine oysters in a tin.

Preheat the oven to 200°C/Fan 180°C/Gas 6 and line a baking sheet with non-stick baking paper.

Drain the oysters and dry well on kitchen paper.

Lay the bacon slices on a board and stretch with the back of a knife. Cut each rasher into 3 pieces.

Wrap a piece of bacon around each oyster, making sure the join is underneath, and sit them on the prepared baking sheet.

Bake in the preheated oven for about 8–10 minutes, or until the bacon is cooked.

Cool slightly before serving hot secured by cocktail sticks.

Double salmon canapés with horseradish

MAKES 20

1 x thin soft dough baguette

olive oil, for brushing

2 tbsp horseradish sauce

3 large pieces of smoked salmon,
  cut into 2cm (¾ in) squares
  (make sure you have 20)

1 x tub mustard and cress

Smoked salmon pâté

150g (5½ oz) smoked salmon

50g (2 oz) full-fat cream cheese

50g (2 oz) full-fat crème fraîche

1 tsp horseradish sauce

a good dash of Tabasco

1 tbsp lemon juice

To prepare ahead
These can be made and
assembled up to 6 hours
ahead and kept in the fridge.
The crostini can be made and
frozen. The pâté can be made
up to 2 days ahead and kept
in the fridge.

To cook in the Aga
Slide the baking sheet on the
floor of the roasting oven for
about 4 minutes on each side
until golden.

*A striking canapé, this is smoked salmon pâté alongside
a good slice of smoked salmon. These look very attractive
served all on one platter. Alternatively serve as a starter on
large bruschetta. Soft dough baguettes are very, very thin,
half-cooked sticks and are the perfect size for this recipe.*

To make the crostini, cut the baguette into 20 thin slices and lightly
brush each side with oil. Arrange on a baking sheet and slide under the
grill for about 2 minutes on each side until golden brown and crisp. Set
aside to cool.

To make the smoked salmon pâté, measure the ingredients into a
processor, add some freshly ground black pepper and whiz briefly
until combined (don't let it get too smooth).

Spread some pâté on to one half of each cold crostini – so the top of
the crostini is half covered with pâté and half plain. Spread a little
horseradish on the plain half. Take a square of smoked salmon and
twist it into a little rosette. Sit this on top of the horseradish.

Snip a few cress leaves and sprinkle a line between the rosette and the
pâté and serve.

Pickled herring and beetroot on rye

MAKES 20

10 slices wholegrain rye bread

1 x 200ml tub full-fat crème
  fraîche

1 x 275g jar herrings in dill
  marinade

4 large bulbs cooked beetroot,
  very finely cubed

a few sprigs of fresh dill

To prepare ahead
Can be made up to 3 hours
ahead and kept in the fridge.
Not suitable for freezing.

*Colourful tasty canapés that will happily stay covered in the
fridge for up to three hours. Wholegrain rye bread is lighter
than Pumpernickel rye bread. The herrings come in jars
and can usually be found alongside other fishy things, like
lumpfish roe and pickled mussels, in the supermarket.*

Lay the bread slices on a board. Using a 4cm (1½ in) pastry cutter,
stamp out 2 rounds from each slice of bread.

Spread the rye rounds with a little crème fraîche.

Cut the herrings into 1cm (½ in) pieces and sit on top of the crème
fraîche (slightly to one side).

Spoon a few pieces of chopped beetroot on to the rye rounds beside
the fish and garnish with a small sprig of dill.

Serve cold with a glass of chilled fizz!

First courses

Country vegetable soup

25g (1 oz) butter

2 medium leeks, sliced

350g (12 oz) celeriac, peeled and
cut into small cubes

250g (9 oz) potato, peeled and cut
into small cubes

850ml (1½ pints) chicken stock

150ml (¼ pint) milk

1 tsp Dijon mustard

a little double cream

1 tbsp snipped fresh chives, to
serve

To prepare ahead
Can be made up to 2 days
ahead. Freezes well.

To cook in the Aga
Bring to the boil on the
boiling plate, cover and
transfer to the simmering
oven for about 30 minutes.

---

*Farm shops are a great source of reasonably priced celeriac
and they make a beautiful soup with leeks and potato. Be
more generous with the cream for a special occasion. Perfect
for any lunch or as a starter on a cold winter's day – and good
to take with you on a picnic or on a cold day of watching
sport or racing.*

Heat the butter in a large saucepan. Add the leeks and fry for a few
minutes. Add the celeriac and potato and fry for a few more minutes
until starting to soften.

Add the stock and season with salt and pepper. Bring up to the boil,
cover and simmer on the hob for about 20 minutes until the vegetables
are just soft.

Ladle the soup into a processor and whiz until smooth.

Return to the pan, add the milk and Dijon mustard and bring back to
the boil. Check the seasoning.

Serve piping hot – to make it look extra special add a swirl of double
cream and a few chives just before serving.

Smoked haddock soup

SERVES 6 – 8

1 large onion, finely chopped

350g (12 oz) potatoes, peeled
weight, finely chopped

2 tbsp olive oil

600ml (1 pint) milk

350g (12 oz) smoked haddock,
skinned and finely diced

2 medium tomatoes, skinned,
de-seeded and finely chopped

4 tbsp double cream

a good grating of nutmeg

a dash of Tabasco

2 large tbsp chopped fresh
flat-leaf parsley

To prepare ahead
Can be made up to a day
ahead and reheated in a pan.
Freezes well.

To cook in the Aga
Cook the onion and potatoes
covered in the simmering
oven for about 20 minutes.

*Before a Sunday roast, serve the soup in smallish, piping hot
soup bowls. The tomatoes add an extra dimension and colour
– and do add a little more cream, if preferred.*

Measure the onion and potatoes into a large saucepan. Add the oil and
fry for a minute over a high heat.

Pour over 300ml boiling water, lower the heat, cover and cook for
about 20 minutes until the vegetables are really soft.

Whiz until smooth with a hand blender or mash with a potato masher.

Pour the milk into a pan, bring to the boil, and then add the haddock.
Simmer gently for about 4 minutes.

Add the haddock and milk to the mashed vegetables, stirring gradually
until combined.

Season with salt and pepper, and add the tomatoes, cream, nutmeg,
Tabasco and 1 tablespoon of parsley.

Serve hot with the remaining parsley as a garnish.

Pea and mint soup

SERVES 6

225g (8 oz) butter

1 large onion, roughly chopped

1kg (2 lb 4 oz) frozen petit pois

850ml (1½ pints) hot chicken or
   vegetable stock

a large bunch of fresh mint

2–3 tbsp mint jelly

a little crème fraîche, to serve

To prepare ahead
Can be made up to a day
ahead and reheated in a pan.
Freezes well.

To cook in the Aga
Cook on the boiling plate
(not in the simmering oven
otherwise the peas will lose
their colour).

*No better soup flavour and no better soup colour. When we
were photographing this soup for the book, the team voted it
the very best soup anyone had tasted for yonks!*

Melt the butter in a large saucepan over a high heat. Add the onion
and fry for about 5 minutes, stirring. Add the peas and fry for a further
couple of minutes. Pour in the stock and bring to the boil.

Remove the leaves from the mint stalks and set them aside. Add the
stalks to the pan and bring back to the boil. Cover and simmer for
about 5–8 minutes, or until the peas are tender.

Stir in the jelly, remove and discard the mint stalks and stir in the mint
leaves. Spoon into a processor and whiz until smooth.

Return to the pan, season with salt and pepper and serve hot or cold,
garnished with a swirl of crème fraîche.

Smoked salmon mousse with cucumber and dill

SERVES 12

350g (12 oz) good quality smoked salmon trimmings

300ml (½ pint) pouring double cream

3 tbsp lemon juice

2 tsp creamed horseradish

1 tsp tomato purée

a good dash of Tabasco

1 packet fresh dill, finely chopped

1 cucumber

salad dressing

a handful of mixed salad leaves

12 small slices of smoked salmon

1 tub mustard and cress

To prepare ahead
The mousses can be made completely up to 2 days ahead. The cucumber salad can be made up to 6 hours ahead – add the dressing and seasoning just before serving. The plates can be arranged up to 6 hours ahead and chilled until served. Not suitable for freezing.

A very attractive first course. If you don't have metal rings, take two dessertspoons of the mousse and carefully shape into oval quenelles and arrange on the salad leaves. Then pile diced cucumber in the centre and some cress on top. Smoked salmon trimmings are usually found vacuum packed in the supermarket salmon section.

Line a baking tray with cling film. Arrange 12 x 7cm (2¾ in) metal rings on the baking tray.

Measure the smoked salmon trimmings into a processor and whiz briefly – just enough to be the size of peppercorns (do not over chop). Add 100ml of the pouring cream and whiz again until combined.

Tip into a bowl, stir in the lemon juice, horseradish, tomato purée, Tabasco and half the chopped dill. Season with black pepper and stir to combine.

Lightly whip the remaining cream and fold it into the bowl.

Spoon into the metal rings and level the tops. Cover each one with cling film and leave in the fridge to set overnight.

Cut the cucumber in half lengthways and, using a teaspoon, scoop out the seeds and discard. Chop the flesh very finely into neat cubes. Tip into a bowl, add a little salad dressing, just to coat, and season with salt and pepper. Stir in the remaining chopped dill.

To serve, place a few salad leaves on twelve individual plates (or on a large platter) and dress with some salad dressing. Sit the salmon mousses on top and carefully remove the rings and cling film. Spoon a little cucumber salad on top of each mousse and arrange a small rosette or ruffle of smoked salmon on top of the cucumber. Sprinkle with snipped cress.

Serve with small bread rolls.

Roasted beetroot and goat's cheese bruschetta

SERVES 6

200g (7 oz) firm goat's cheese in a roll

2 raw medium beetroot

4 tbsp olive oil, plus extra for drizzling

3 large red onions, thinly sliced

1 tbsp brown sugar

1 tbsp fresh thyme leaves, chopped

1 tbsp balsamic glaze, plus extra for drizzling

½ x part-baked ciabatta loaf

1 x 85g packet mixed green salad leaves

salad dressing, to serve

To prepare ahead
The roasted beetroot, bruschetta and marmalade can be made up to a day ahead. Not suitable for freezing.

To cook in the Aga
Roast the beetroot on the floor of the roasting oven for about 15 minutes. Cook the onions on the boiling plate for 5 minutes, then cover and transfer to the simmering oven for about 20 minutes. Cook the ciabatta on the floor of the roasting oven for about 3 minutes on each side. Arrange the goat's cheese and return to the top of the roasting oven for a further 5 minutes.

If you are not going to use the other half of the ciabatta straight away, wrap it in foil and freeze. Balsamic glaze comes in a plastic squeezable bottle and is thicker than balsamic vinegar.

Preheat the oven to 200°C/Fan 180°C/Gas 6 and line two baking sheets with non-stick paper.

Put the goat's cheese in the freezer for 30 minutes. Shave off the ends, if necessary, and then slice into 6 – it is easier to slice with a serrated knife.

Peel the raw beetroot (using gloves) and slice into 1cm (½ in) dice. Tip into a bowl and toss the cubes in 2 tablespoons of the oil and season. Scatter on one of the prepared baking sheets and roast in the preheated oven for 25 minutes until lightly golden.

Measure 2 tablespoons of the oil into a frying pan. Add the red onions and stir over a high heat for 3–4 minutes. Cover with a lid, lower the heat and simmer for 15 minutes until completely soft.

Remove the lid and increase the heat. Add the sugar and thyme. Fry until the onions have caramelised and then add the balsamic glaze.

Slice the ciabatta into 6 x 2cm (¾ in) slices. Brush each side with a little olive oil and arrange up one end of the other baking sheet. Slide into the oven for about 5 minutes, or until the bread is lightly pale golden.

Remove from the oven and put the goat's cheese slices on the other side of the baking sheet. Return to the oven for 10 minutes, or until the cheese is just melting.

Spoon the onion marmalade on top of the bruschetta and arrange in the centre of a large plate. Sit the warm goat's cheese on top.

Toss the salad leaves in a little dressing and place a handful on top of each slice of cheese.

Drizzle some olive oil and balsamic glaze around the edge of the plates and arrange the roasted beetroot around the bruschetta.

Serve warm.

The ultimate all seasons salad

SERVES 6

3 Little Gem lettuces

1 x 100g packet mixed rocket and chard

1 x 70g packet lamb's lettuce

6 small cherry tomatoes

1 x 70g packet Milano salami slices

6 slices Parma ham

100g (4 oz) black seedless grapes

1 x 200g jar char-grilled artichokes in oil, each cut in half

150g (5½ oz) good feta cheese

50g (2 oz) pine nuts

a few shavings of Parmesan cheese

Honey and mustard dressing

1 tbsp runny honey

1 tbsp Dijon mustard

6 tbsp extra virgin olive oil

3 tbsp white wine vinegar

1 tsp caster sugar

To prepare ahead
Cover with cling film after adding the Parmesan and keep in the fridge for up to 3 hours. Dress before serving. Not suitable for freezing.

Great to serve on a huge flat plate or tray – about 35cm (14 in) round – then everyone can share and help themselves. Looks simply stunning and you can vary the ingredients according to what is in season and available.

To assemble the salad, arrange all the salad leaves over the base of the platter. Slice the tomatoes in half and arrange over the leaves.

Fold the salami into cone shapes and arrange over the top.

Trim any excess fat from the Parma ham and cut each slice in half. Pinch into little piles and arrange on the salad, along with the grapes and artichoke pieces.

Crumble the feta into large pieces and sprinkle on to the arrangement.

Season with a little salt and pepper, and then scatter over the pine nuts and Parmesan shavings.

For the dressing, measure the ingredients into a bowl and whisk by hand until smooth. Season with salt and pepper.

Drizzle the dressing over the salad just before serving.

Spectacular trout and caper first course

SERVES 6

balsamic glaze, for drizzling

450g (1 lb) smoked trout

1 large red onion, finely sliced

1 x 200ml tub crème fraîche

3 tbsp chopped fresh dill

a dash of lemon juice

6 lemon wedges

6 tbsp mini capers

To prepare ahead
Can be assembled up to 8 hours ahead. Not suitable for freezing.

This is such a simple first course but it looks absolutely stunning. Balsamic glaze can be bought in a bottle in the supermarkets and is similar to the ones used in restaurants – the plastic bottle is so easy to squeeze and create zigzag patterns. Cold smoked trout looks like smoked salmon but has a more delicate flavour.

Take 6 white starter plates and drizzle a zigzag pattern across the middle of each plate with the balsamic glaze.

Divide the trout into 6. Take 1 portion and curl it into a pile and sit it just off-centre on each plate. Arrange a few slices of red onion next to the trout.

Mix the crème fraîche with the dill and lemon juice, and season with salt and pepper. Spoon some on to each plate opposite the salmon so you have a rough triangle shape on the plate.

Arrange a lemon wedge at one end of each plate and scatter a tablespoon of capers around the edge.

Serve with brown bread and butter.

Baked stuffed mushrooms with three cheeses

SERVES 6

6 Portobello mushrooms

3 tbsp olive oil

12 rashers streaky bacon, roughly chopped

250g (9 oz) full-fat cream cheese

50g (2 oz) Stilton cheese, grated

1 medium egg, beaten

100g (4 oz) Emmental cheese, grated

dusting of paprika, to serve

To prepare ahead
Can be assembled up to 8 hours ahead and cooked and served immediately. Not suitable for freezing.

To cook in the Aga
Cook on the top set of runners in the roasting oven for about 12 minutes.

This makes a very good first course, especially if you have chosen a lighter main course. It is also a good way of using up various cheeses left after a party.

Preheat the oven to 220°C/Fan 200°C/Gas 7 and line a baking sheet with non-stick paper or foil.

Remove the stalks from the mushrooms and season with salt and pepper.

Heat the oil in a frying pan and fry the mushrooms over a high heat for 2 minutes on each side. Transfer to the lined baking sheet, gill side up.

Add the bacon to the pan and fry over a high heat until crisp. Spoon on to kitchen paper to cool.

Measure the cream cheese into a bowl, add the Stilton and egg and beat together using a wooden spoon until combined. Stir in the cooled bacon and half the Emmental cheese, and season with pepper (no salt needed).

Divide the mixture equally into six and spoon on top of the mushrooms. Sprinkle with the remaining cheese and a dusting of paprika.

Cook in the preheated oven for 12–15 minutes until golden on top.

Serve hot with salad leaves.

Quick liver pâté with pistachios

SERVES 6 - 8

100g (4 oz) soft butter

1 small onion, finely chopped

350g (12 oz) fresh chicken livers

2 tbsp Madeira or sherry

4 tbsp chopped fresh parsley

1 tbsp double cream

25g (1 oz) pistachio nuts, roughly chopped

To prepare ahead
Can be made up to 2 days ahead and kept in the fridge. Freezes well.

A very quick and simple pâté – no cooking in the oven needed. The pistachio nuts give a wonderful colour and flavour.

You will need 6 x size 1 ramekins or an 850ml (1½ pint) dish.

Melt half the butter in a frying pan over a low heat. Add the onion and cook for about 5 minutes until tender. Using a slotted spoon, transfer to a plate.

Add the livers to the pan and fry over a high heat for about 3–4 minutes until just cooked. Add to the plate with the onion and leave to cool.

Place the onion and livers in a processor and whiz until coarse. Add the Madeira, parsley, double cream, half the pistachio nuts and the remaining soft butter. Whiz again until smooth.

Spoon into the ramekins or serving dish and sprinkle with the remaining nuts. Chill for 6 hours.

Serve with toast and chutney, if liked.

Prawn cocktail with avocado

SERVES 6

300g (10 oz) cooked peeled North
  Atlantic prawns, drained and
  dried

2 ripe medium avocadoes

juice of 1 lemon

1 x 85g packet mixed lettuce
  leaves

6 large shell-on cooked king
  prawns

1 lemon, cut into 6 wedges

Cocktail sauce

8 tbsp light mayonnaise

4 tbsp crème fraîche

6 tbsp ketchup

2 tbsp creamed horseradish

1½ tsp tomato purée

the juice of ½ lemon

a dash of sugar

To prepare ahead
The sauce can be made up
to 3 days ahead. The dish
can be assembled up to 4
hours ahead. Not suitable for
freezing.

---

*A classic 70s recipe but with the addition of avocado –
it deserves a comeback!*

To make the sauce, mix all the ingredients together in a bowl and
season with salt and pepper.

Stir in the peeled prawns.

Cut the avocadoes into small dice, toss in the lemon juice and season
with pepper.

Divide the lettuce between 6 glasses and arrange the avocado on top.
Spoon the prawn mixture over the top and garnish each glass with a
large prawn.

Serve with a small lemon wedge and brown bread and butter.

Ceviche

SERVES 6

3 scallops, each sliced in two
   horizontally

200g (7 oz) squid

100g (4 oz) brill or turbot,
   skinned and cut into 2cm
   (¾ in) pieces

the juice of 2 limes

1–2 green chillies, finely chopped

½ small red onion, finely
   chopped

1 large avocado, finely chopped

3 tomatoes, seeds removed and
   finely sliced

125ml (4 fl oz) olive oil

2 tbsp chopped fresh coriander
   leaves

To prepare ahead
The platter can be arranged
up to 4 hours ahead. Not
suitable for freezing.

---

*Ceviche – marinated raw fish – is a very smart first course
that is popular in Latin America, especially in Peru and
Mexico. The lime juice 'cooks' the raw fish and turns the flesh
opaque so use only the freshest fish. If you enjoy sushi give
this a try.*

Measure the scallops, squid and brill into a bowl and pour over the
lime juice. Turn so all the fish is coated and transfer to the fridge for
about 5 hours, or until opaque.

Measure the chilli, onion, avocado and tomatoes into a bowl and
season with salt and pepper. Add the oil.

Drain the fish from the lime juice and add the juice to the bowl with
the vegetables.

Arrange the fish on 6 small plates and spoon the vegetables and juices
over the top.

Scatter with the chopped coriander leaves and serve chilled with brown
bread.

Beef

Beef roasting chart

Few people can resist beef roasted to perfection. We like it fairly rare. On the bone it cooks and tastes best but boned and rolled is far easier to carve. It will take a little longer to cook off the bone as it will be a thicker, denser joint.

Bring the beef joint to room temperature before roasting. Lightly oil the fatty skin, season with salt and pepper and stand in a roasting tin.

The timings given below are a guide, depending on the size of your joint. Bear in mind that a thicker joint weighing the same amount as a longer, thinner joint will take a bit more time to roast. Also, ovens vary a lot in efficiency and thermostats are not always accurate. Using a meat thermometer will eliminate the guesswork, but make sure the thermometer is not touching a bone when you test the meat. The internal temperature of the meat will continue to rise by as much as ten degrees when rested, so remove the joint a little before your required temperature.

Start roasting at 220°C/Fan 200°C/Gas 7 to seal the meat and then after 20 minutes lower the temperature to 180°C/ Fan 160°C/Gas 4.

	TOTAL ROASTING TIME	INTERNAL TEMP
Rare	20 minutes per 450g (1 lb) plus 20 minutes	60°C
Medium	25 minutes per 450g (1 lb) plus 20 minutes	70°C
Well done	30 minutes per 450g (1 lb) plus 20 minutes	75–80°C

* For *Roast rib of beef* see page 33
* For fillet of beef see page 177
* For *Slow-roast silverside* see page 40

Roast rib of beef

SERVES 6-8

approx 2.7kg (6 lb) rib joint, prime rib or wing rib beef

2 large onions, cut into wedges

To prepare ahead
The joint should be cooked and served but it is delicious cold the next day if you have leftovers. Not suitable for freezing.

To cook in the Aga
Cook in the roasting oven for 12 minutes per 450g (1 lb).

Roast rib of beef is the preferred joint of many butchers for a Sunday lunch – order it well in advance and ask for it to be well-hung (this increases the flavour). It is much fattier than a fillet of beef and, therefore, it has a lot more flavour. If you prefer to have the rib boned before you roast it, it will be easier to carve but not look so spectacular. The cooking time will be about the same, though. (See the beef roasting chart on page 31 for internal temperatures.)

Preheat the oven to 220°C/Fan 200°C/Gas 7 and bring the beef to room temperature for 30 minutes before roasting.

Arrange the onion pieces in a large roasting tin and sit the rib on top. Transfer to the oven and roast in the preheated oven for 20 minutes, or until brown.

Turn the oven down to 180°C/Fan 160°C/Gas 4 and roast the rib joint for 20 minutes per 450g (1 lb) (including the initial 20 minutes). (For example, the second roasting of a 2.7kg/6 lb rib joint should be 1 hour 40 minutes.)

Remove the meat from the oven and from its roasting tin. Discard the onions and wrap the beef in foil to keep hot while resting. Allow to rest for about 20 minutes.

Meanwhile, make the gravy (see page 146–7).

Serve the rib with *Yorkshire pudding* (see page 141), *Perfect roast potatoes* (see page 140) and *Horseradish sauce* (see page 150).

Cottage pie with thyme and mushrooms

SERVES 6

675g (1½ lb) minced beef

2 large onions, chopped

40g (1½ oz) plain flour

150ml (¼ pint) Port

1 tbsp Worcestershire sauce

2 tsp redcurrant jelly

2 tsp fresh thyme leaves, chopped

500g (1 lb 2 oz) brown chestnut
    mushrooms, sliced

a dash of gravy browning,
    optional

1kg (2lb 4 oz) King Edward
    potatoes, peeled and cut into
    4cm (1½ in) cubes

knob of butter

a little milk

To prepare ahead
The whole dish can be made
up to a day ahead and kept in
the fridge. Freezes well.

To cook in the Aga
Cook the mince in the
simmering oven, covered,
for about 1 hour 15 minutes.
Cook the completed dish on
the top set of runners in the
roasting oven for about 30
minutes.

---

*Cottage pie is an all-time favourite and the one dish that
everyone in the family, young and old, will enjoy. The Port
gives it a bit of a punch but if you are cooking the pie for very
young children, you can replace it with beef stock.*

Preheat the oven to 180°C/Fan 160°C/Gas 4. You will need a shallow 2
litre (3½ pint) ovenproof dish.

Heat a large flameproof casserole over a high heat and brown the
minced beef all over. Make sure you break up the mince into small
pieces as it browns. Add the onions and continue to fry for a few
minutes.

Sprinkle over the flour, stir and blend in the Port, and bring to the boil,
stirring until thickened. Add the Worcestershire sauce, redcurrant jelly,
thyme and season with salt and pepper.

Stir in the mushrooms, cover with a lid and cook in the preheated oven
for about an hour or until tender.

Remove from the oven, add a little gravy browning if using, and check
the seasoning. Spoon into the ovenproof dish and leave to cool slightly.

Meanwhile, put the potatoes into a large saucepan, cover with water,
add salt and bring to the boil. Boil until completely tender.

Drain the potatoes and return them to the pan. Push to one side and
add the butter and milk. Heat and then mash with a potato masher
until smooth.

Spread the mashed potato over the mince so it is completely covered
and then drag a fork along the top.

Cook in the preheated oven for about 30–35 minutes until lightly
golden and bubbling around the sides.

Simple beef cassoulet

SERVES 6 – 8

2 tbsp oil

1kg (2 lb 4 oz) braising beef,
   cut into 2cm (¾ in) cubes

3 large onions, sliced

2 sticks celery, sliced

2 cloves garlic, crushed

25g (1 oz) plain flour

550ml (19 fl oz) cold beef stock

2 tbsp sun-dried tomato paste

1 tbsp balsamic vinegar

2 tsp soy sauce

1 tsp brown sugar

2 x 400g can butterbeans, drained

fresh parsley, chopped
   (to garnish)

To prepare ahead
Can be made up to 2 days
ahead – but only add the
beans when you are reheating.
Freezes well without the beans.

To cook in the Aga
Bring to the boil on the
boiling plate. Cover and
transfer to the simmering
oven for about 2 hours. Add
the beans and return to the
simmering oven for a further
30 minutes.

*This is great for an informal lunch in winter. If you have
very young guests, add some baked beans instead of the
butter beans.*

Preheat the oven to 160°C/Fan 140°C/Gas 3.

Heat 1 tablespoon of the oil in a large flameproof casserole, add the
beef and brown until sealed. You may need to do this in batches.
Remove from the pan and set aside.

Heat the remaining oil in the pan, add the onions and celery and fry
for 5 minutes until starting soften. Add the garlic and continue to fry
for a minute until starting to brown slightly.

Meanwhile, measure the flour into a bowl and mix with a little of the
cold stock to make a smooth paste.

Return the meat to the pan, add the remaining stock, the sun-dried
tomato paste, vinegar, soy and sugar. Bring to the boil.

Add a few tablespoons of the hot liquid to the flour paste, stir to loosen
and then pour into the pan. Bring to the boil, stirring until thick, and
season with salt and pepper. Cover and transfer to the preheated oven
for about 2 hours or until the beef is just tender.

Add the beans and return to the oven for a further 30 minutes.

Serve hot sprinkled with parsley with some green veg.

Beef Wellington

SERVES 6–8

1.5kg (3 lb 5 oz) centre cut fillet of beef

2 tbsp olive oil

1 x 375g packet all-butter puff pastry

1 medium egg, beaten

Fillet topping and luxury gravy

1 tbsp olive oil

2 large onions, roughly chopped

1 tbsp brown sugar

2 tbsp balsamic vinegar

25g (1 oz) butter

3 level tbsp plain flour

300ml (½ pint) red wine, reduced to 150ml (¼ pint)

600ml (1pint) hot beef stock

2 tsp redcurrant jelly

1 tbsp Worcestershire sauce

a dash of gravy browning, optional

This makes a spectacular Sunday lunch. All the preparation, including the gravy, can be done ahead. Timing is crucial, though. The times given here are for medium rare beef.

Preheat the oven to 220°C/Fan 200°C/Gas 7 and grease a roasting tin.

Trim off any excess fat or tissue from the outside of the fillet and season with salt and pepper.

Place a large frying pan over a high heat, add the oil and brown the fillet on all sides. Lift out on to the roasting tin and roast in the preheated oven for 20–22 minutes according to the thickness of the fillet. Remove from the oven and leave to become cold.

To make the fillet topping and luxury gravy, place a tablespoon of oil in the same frying pan and add the onions and brown sugar. Cook slowly, turning until caramelised. Stir in the balsamic vinegar and season with salt and pepper.

Put half of the onion mixture to one side to spread on top of the fillet before wrapping in pastry and use the other half in the pan to make the luxury gravy.

Add the butter to the pan and melt over a medium heat. Sprinkle over the flour and blend well. Whisk in the reduced red wine, the hot stock, redcurrant jelly and Worcestershire sauce. Bring up to the boil and simmer for 1 minute before straining into a jug. Add a little gravy browning, if liked.

Roll the pastry out on a floured work surface to make a large oblong shape about 50 x 35cm (20 x 14 in). Cut about 5cm (2 in) from the long end to use for decorating. This should leave enough to wrap the fillet in.

Spread the reserved onions on top of the cold fillet. Wrap the beef in the pastry, sealing the long side and ends with beaten egg.

continued

Lift the beef Wellington on to a baking sheet and brush with the egg. Twist the reserved piece of pastry and lay it across the top to decorate. Chill in the fridge until ready to bake.

Remove from the fridge 2 hours before baking and glaze with beaten egg again. Preheat the oven to 220°C/Fan 200°C/Gas 7.

Bake for about 25–30 minutes until the pastry is golden brown and crisp. Rest for 15 minutes loosely covered with foil.

Carve the beef and serve with the reheated gravy and horseradish sauce.

Cornish pie

SERVES 8

Filling

450g (1 lb) minced beef

1 large onion, finely chopped

175g (6 oz) peeled potatoes, very finely diced

100g (4 oz) peeled carrots, very finely diced

100g (4 oz) peeled swede, very finely diced

2 tbsp beef stock

Pastry

350g (12 oz) strong white flour

100g (4 oz) lard, cubed

15g (½ oz) spread for baking or soft butter

150ml (¼ pint) water

1 medium egg, beaten

To prepare ahead
Can be made up to a day ahead and reheated in a low oven. Freezes well.

To cook in the Aga
Bake on the grid shelf on the floor of the roasting oven for about 30 minutes. Slide the cold sheet on the second set of runners, remove the grid shelf and cook on the floor of the roasting oven for a further 10 minutes. Transfer to the simmering oven and bake for a final 30 minutes.

The pastry used in this pie is typically Cornish – made with strong white flour, it is short and crumbly. An old-fashioned pie, the meat filling is firm and dense, and it is delicious served with chutney.

Preheat the oven to 220°C/Fan 200°C/Gas 7. You will need a roasting tin or Swiss roll tin that is 33 x 23cm (13 x 9 in).

Tip all the filling ingredients into a bowl, mix together and season really well with salt and pepper.

To make the pastry, measure the flour, lard and spread into a processor and whiz until it looks like breadcrumbs. Add the water and whiz again to combine. Remove from the processor and gently knead the dough until smooth.

Roll out two-thirds of the pastry into a rectangle shape. Line the base of the roasting tin with the pastry and spoon all the filling mixture on top. Pat down with a spoon so it is even and filling the corners. Level the top.

Roll the remaining pastry into the same shape to form a lid. Damp the edges with water and cover the pastry. Press down and crimp the edges. Using a knife, make three slits in the middle of the pastry to allow the steam to escape. Brush the top with the beaten egg.

Bake in the preheated oven for 35–40 minutes until lightly golden, then reduce the oven temperature to 180°C/Fan 160°C/Gas 4 and cook for a further 30 minutes.

Slice into squares and serve hot with gravy (see page 146–7) or cold for a picnic.

Slow-roast silverside with English roots and gravy

SERVES 8

900g (2 lb) joint of silverside

1 large onion, cut into large pieces

3 cloves garlic

450ml (16 fl oz) beef stock

English roots

4 large potatoes, peeled and evenly cubed

3 medium carrots, peeled and cut slightly smaller than the potatoes

4 onions, each cut into 6 wedges

3 large parsnips, peeled and cut into cubes the same size as the potatoes

2 tablespoons oil

1 tablespoon honey

Beurre manié

25g (1 oz) butter, softened

25g (1 oz) flour

Slow roasting more reasonable cuts of beef means they are bound to be tender and the timing doesn't have to be spot on. Even if you cook the dish for an hour longer than the recipe requires, it will still be delicious. You can use brisket here, if you prefer. Beurre manié (equal quantities of soft butter and flour blended to a paste) gives this dish a lovely, smooth gravy.

Preheat the oven to 160°C/Fan 140°C/Gas 3 and bring the joint to room temperature before roasting.

Massage the meat with oil and season generously with black pepper.

Place a large flameproof casserole over a high heat and brown the joint on all sides. Transfer to a plate. Take off the heat and add the onion and garlic to the dish and sit the joint on top. Pour the stock over the meat, cover tightly with a lid or foil and cook in the preheated oven for about 3 hours until tender.

To make the English roots put all the vegetables in a large saucepan, cover with salted water and bring to the boil. Boil for 5 minutes and then drain.

If you have two ovens, heat the oil in a large roasting tin, and then add the roots and roast at 200°C/Fan 180°C/Gas 6 for about 45 minutes or until tender (pouring the honey over the roots 20 minutes before the end of the cooking time). If you only have one oven, wait until the joint is cooked and then set it aside to rest. Increase the oven temperature and cook as above. The meat can rest for 45–60 minutes wrapped in foil and covered in a thick, clean tea towel to keep warm.

Place a sieve over a large saucepan and pour in the stock and juices from the joint. Bring to the boil.

Meanwhile, make the beurre manié by mixing the butter and flour together to form a paste. Whisk into the stock and allow to thicken. Check for seasoning. Add a touch of gravy browning if you like a dark gravy.

Carve the meat and serve with the roots and gravy.

To prepare ahead
The joint should be cooked and then served but it is delicious cold the next day if you have leftovers. The roots can be cooked up to 6 hours ahead and reheated in a very hot oven to cook through. Not suitable for freezing.

To cook in the Aga
See slow cooking times on page 223 for the joint. For the English roots, cook on the floor of the roasting oven for about 30 minutes.

Slow roasting times

All at 160°C/Fan 140°C/Gas 3

Brown the joint first then cook for:

450g (1 lb)	2 hours
900g (2 lb)	3 hours
1.3kg (3 lb)	4 hours
1.8kg (4 lb)	5 hours

Steak, kidney and mushroom pie

SERVES 6

750g (1 lb 10 oz) skirt beef, diced into 4cm (1½ in) cubes

250g (9 oz) beef kidney, cut into 1cm (½ in) cubes

50g (2 oz) flour

25g (1 oz) butter

2 large onions, chopped

2 tbsp oil

300ml (½ pint) red wine

300ml (½ pint) beef stock

1 tbsp redcurrant jelly

1 sprig of thyme

2 bay leaves

300g (10 oz) chestnut mushrooms

1 x 500g packet all-butter puff pastry

1 medium egg, beaten

If I'm cooking steak and kidney for a really large gathering – say eighteen people – rather than make huge pies, I cook one large batch of steak and kidney and make individual pie tops. I cook the pastry in advance on a baking sheet and then just reheat them to serve on the stew.

Preheat the oven to 160°C/Fan 140°C/Gas 3. You will need a 1.2 litre (2 pint) pie dish.

Tip the beef and kidney cubes into a bowl, sprinkle in the flour, season with salt and pepper and toss with your hands so the meat becomes coated.

Melt the butter in a saucepan over a high heat, add the onions and fry for a minute. Cover and cook over a low heat for about 15 minutes until soft.

Heat the oil in a large flameproof casserole over a high heat and brown the beef and kidneys on all sides (you may need to do this in batches).

Sprinkle over any remaining flour from the bowl, add the onions and stir in the wine and stock. Bring to the boil. Add the redcurrant jelly and herbs and season with salt and pepper. Bring back to the boil, cover with a lid and cook in the preheated oven for about 2 hours.

Add the mushrooms and continue to cook for a further 30 minutes, or until the meat is tender.

Remove and discard the herbs and spoon the casserole into the pie dish, keeping back some of the gravy to serve separately. Set aside to cool.

Meanwhile, increase the oven temperature to 220°C/Fan 200°C/Gas 7.

Roll out the pastry 4cm (1½ in) larger than the top of the pie dish (sit the dish on top and cut around it). (You will have some pastry left which you can freeze for another day.)

continued

Brush a little water along the lip of the pie dish. Slice thin strips from the edge of the pastry and lay these along the top of the lip. Brush these with water and then place the rolled-out pastry along the top. Trim and seal the edges of the pastry and then brush the top with beaten egg.

Cook the pie in the oven for about 30–40 minutes, or until golden and crisp.

Serve piping hot with some green veg and the reserved gravy.

Boiled beef and carrots with mustard sauce

SERVES 6-8

1.5kg (3 lb 5 oz) boned and rolled
   salted silverside
500g (1 lb 2 oz) baby carrots
500g (1 lb 2 oz) shallots, peeled
1 celery heart, sliced thickly

Mustard sauce
50g (2 oz) butter
50g (2 oz) flour
300ml (½ pint) reserved stock
150ml (¼ pint) milk
150ml (¼ pint) double cream
1 level tbsp mustard powder
2-3 tbsp white wine vinegar
1½ tbsp caster sugar
1½ tbsp Dijon mustard

To prepare ahead
The beef and vegetables can be
made up to a day ahead. They
should be gently reheated on
the hob in their stock for an
hour before removing to a
serving plate and making the
sauce. Not suitable for freezing.

To cook in the Aga
Bring to the boil on the boiling
plate, cover and transfer to the
simmering oven for about 3
hours, add the vegetables and
cook for a further hour.

Salt beef is rarely available in supermarkets but good butchers often have it in the winter months. It is best to order ahead as it may not be a joint that your butcher stocks. Freeze any leftover stock, or keep it in the fridge, to use in other beef dishes or to make gravy (see page 146-7).

Soak the beef overnight in cold water, if necessary – ask your butcher or check the packaging.

Place the beef in a deep saucepan and cover with cold water. Bring up to the boil, cover with a lid and simmer on the hob very, very gently for 2 hours.

Add the carrots, shallots and celery to the saucepan and continue to simmer for 45-60 minutes until the beef is tender and the vegetables are soft.

Remove the meat and vegetables and arrange on a serving plate covered with foil to keep warm. Pour 300ml of the stock into a measuring jug.

To make the sauce, melt the butter in a saucepan, add the flour and stir together over a high heat for 1 minute. Whisk in the reserved stock, milk and double cream. Bring up to the boil.

Mix the mustard powder and vinegar together in a small bowl. Add to the sauce, stirring, and bring back to the boil. Add the caster sugar and Dijon mustard and check the seasoning.

Pour the sauce into a jug and serve with the beef and vegetables.

Oxtail stew

SERVES 6

2 oxtails

2 large onions, thickly sliced

3 large carrots, thickly sliced

8 sticks celery, thickly sliced

1 fat clove garlic, crushed

50g (2 oz) flour

1 litre (1¾ pints) beef stock

2 tbsp tomato purée

2 bay leaves

1 tsp fresh thyme leaves, chopped

2–3 tbsp balsamic vinegar

2 tbsp chopped fresh parsley

To prepare ahead
Best made the day before but can be made up to 2 days ahead. Reheat and serve as detailed (right). Not suitable for freezing.

To cook in the Aga
Bring to the boil on the boiling plate, cover and transfer to the simmering oven for about 5–6 hours. To reheat, bring to the boil, cover and transfer to the simmering oven for about an hour.

This recipe needs to be made a day ahead so that the fat, which will rise to the surface when it has cooled, can be removed before serving. Oxtails are available from all good butchers and some supermarkets sell them, too. This stew is delicious served with a mash made from root vegetables, like parsnip and potato, or celeriac and potato, and traditional winter vegetables.

Preheat the oven to 140°C/Fan 120°C/Gas 2 and trim any excess fat from the oxtail joints.

Place a large flameproof casserole over a medium heat and brown the joints really well on all sides. Transfer to a plate.

Add the vegetables and garlic to the pan and cook over a low heat for about 5 minutes until starting to soften.

Sprinkle in the flour and stir to coat the vegetables.

Gradually add the stock, stirring, and then the tomato purée, bay leaves and thyme, and season with salt and pepper. Bring to the boil, stirring, and then return the oxtail to the pan.

Cover with a lid, transfer to the preheated oven and cook for about 4–5 hours or until the meat is tender.

Leave to cool overnight.

Preheat the oven to 140°C/Fan 120°C/Gas 2 and remove the excess fat from the top of the cold stew.

Place over a medium heat and bring to the boil. Cover and transfer to the oven, stirring from time to time, for an hour or until hot through.

Remove the bay leaves, stir in the vinegar and serve piping hot sprinkled with parsley.

Chilli con carne

SERVES 6

4 rashers smoked bacon, roughly chopped

1kg (2 lb 4 oz) minced beef

2 large onions, roughly chopped

2 large cloves garlic, crushed

1 red pepper, deseeded and diced

25g (1 oz) plain flour

2 tsp paprika powder

1–2 tsp hot chilli powder

2 x 400g can chopped tomatoes

300ml (½ pint) beef stock

2 tsp brown sugar

3 tbsp tomato purée

1 x 400g can kidney beans, drained and rinsed

To prepare ahead
Can be made up to 2 days ahead and reheated on the hob or in a low oven to serve. Freezes well cooked.

To cook in the Aga
Bring to the boil on the boiling plate, cover and transfer to the simmering oven for about 2 hours.

Add as much chilli powder as your family enjoy – teenagers seem to like it hot! If you have a really hungry lot, just add another can of kidney beans.

Preheat the oven to 160°C/Fan 140°C/Gas 3.

Place a large flameproof casserole over a high heat. Add the bacon and fry until crisp. Remove from the pan and set aside.

Add the mince to the pan and brown in batches, breaking up the mince into small pieces.

Drain off any fat. Add the onions, garlic and red pepper. Stir for a minute and then return the bacon to the pan.

Sprinkle over the flour and spices and coat the beef mixture. Add the chopped tomatoes, stock, sugar and tomato purée. Bring up to the boil, cover with a lid and place in the preheated oven to simmer for 1½–2 hours until tender. (You can simmer the chilli on the hob if you prefer.) Add the kidney beans 30 minutes before the end of the cooking time.

Serve with rice (see page 166), guacamole, sour cream, tomato salsa, tortilla chips and grated Cheddar.

Beef bourguignon

SERVES 6-8

2 tbsp oil

900g (2 lb) good stewing steak

175g (6 oz) smoked streaky bacon

1 large onion, thickly sliced

2 fat cloves garlic, crushed

450ml (16 fl oz) red wine

40g (1½ oz) flour

4 tbsp brandy

600ml (1 pint) beef stock

1 tsp fresh thyme leaves, chopped

175g (6 oz) chestnut mushrooms

a knob of butter

12 small raw pickling onions

2 tbsp finely chopped fresh parsley

To prepare ahead
Can be made 2 days ahead, adding the mushrooms and onions when reheating in a moderate oven. Freezes well without the mushroom and onion mixture.

To cook in the Aga
Bring to the boil on the boiling plate, cover and transfer to the simmering oven for about 2 hours. Add the fried mushrooms and onions and cook for a further hour in the simmering oven or until completely tender.

This is a real classic French casserole that is wonderfully rich. I always reduce the wine before adding it to the casserole as it greatly improves the flavour and colour.

Preheat the oven to 160°C/Fan 140°C/Gas 3.

Place the oil in a flameproof casserole over a high heat. Dice the beef, add to the pan and brown on all sides (you will need to do this in batches). Transfer the meat to a plate.

Cut the bacon into small pieces and add to the pan with the onion and garlic and fry until the bacon is starting to brown.

In a separate wide-based pan, pour in the wine and boil to reduce by half.

Sprinkle the flour over the onion, bacon and garlic mixture and then pour over the reduced wine, the brandy and half the stock. Stir until combined and thickened, and bring to the boil.

Add the remaining stock, return the meat to the pan, season with salt and pepper and add the thyme. Bring to the boil, cover with a lid and transfer to the preheated oven for about 1½–2 hours.

When the cooking time is almost up, cut the mushrooms in half and fry over a medium heat in another pan with a knob of butter for about 2 minutes. Peel the pickling onions and add them to the pan, tossing together.

Add the mushrooms and onions to the casserole and then continue to cook for a further 40 minutes, or until the meat is completely tender.

Sprinkle with parsley and serve hot from the oven.

Family lasagne

100g (4 oz) smoked bacon lardons

1 tbsp oil

900g (2 lb) minced beef

2 large onions, chopped

2 fat cloves garlic, crushed

40g (1½ oz) flour

2 x 400g can chopped tomatoes

5 tbsp tomato purée

1 tbsp redcurrant jelly

150ml (¼ pint) beef stock

1 tsp fresh thyme leaves, chopped

1 x 375g packet no-cook dried
   lasagne (you won't need it all)

White sauce

75g (3 oz) butter

75g (3 oz) flour

1 litre (1¾ pints) hot milk

50g (2 oz) Parmesan cheese

75g (3 oz) Cheddar cheese

a good grating fresh nutmeg

2 tsp Dijon mustard

To prepare ahead
Can be made up to a day
ahead and kept in the fridge.
Freezes well.

To cook in the Aga
Bring the mince to the boil,
cover and transfer to the
simmering oven for about an
hour. Cook the lasagne on the
second set of runners in the
roasting oven for 45 minutes.

A real family favourite and there's no last-minute carving to do or gravy to make, as there would be with a roast. Just serve it with a salad and maybe some warm garlic bread. I don't use a lot of pasta, as we find most people prefer it not too solid.

Preheat the oven to 160°C/Fan 140°C/Gas 3. You will need a shallow 2.8–3.4 litre (5–6 pint) wide-based ovenproof dish.

First prepare the meat sauce. Place a large flameproof casserole over a high heat and add the bacon. Fry for a few minutes until the fat comes out. Add the oil and mince, and fry quickly until brown all over, breaking up the meat as it cooks.

Add the onions and garlic and fry for a couple of minutes. Sprinkle in the flour and cook for a further minute. Add the chopped tomatoes, tomato purée, redcurrant jelly, stock and thyme leaves. Fry for a few minutes and then season with salt and pepper. Bring to the boil, stirring. Cover and simmer on the hob or transfer to the preheated oven for about 1½ hours, or until tender.

Take out of the oven and turn the temperature up to 190°C/Fan 170°C/Gas 5. If the meat is a little thick add a touch more stock or water.

Meanwhile, to make the white sauce, melt the butter in a saucepan over a medium heat, add the flour and cook for a minute. Pour in the milk, stirring all the time until the milk comes to the boil and thickens. Grate the cheeses and add half of each to the saucepan with the nutmeg and mustard. Season with salt and pepper.

Spoon a layer of the meat sauce into the ovenproof dish and then lay sheets of lasagne over the top (be careful not to overlap the sheets). Spoon a layer of cheese sauce on top. Continue until you have two layers of each. Finish with the cheese sauce and sprinkle with the remaining cheese.

Cook in the preheated oven for about 45–60 minutes or until golden brown and the pasta is tender.

Lamb

Lamb roasting chart

Lamb leg and shoulders are the favourite lamb roasts and both cook on the bone well. Before roasting, dust with seasoning and a smear of oil. Make holes in the skin with a sharp knife and poke a sliver of garlic and a tiny sprig of rosemary into each hole – the flavour will enhance the meat during cooking.

The timings given below are a guide, depending on the size of your joint. Bear in mind that a thicker joint weighing the same amount as a longer, thinner joint will take a bit more time to roast. Also, ovens vary a lot in efficiency and thermostats are not always accurate. Using a meat thermometer will eliminate the guesswork, but make sure the thermometer is not touching a bone when you test the meat. The internal temperature of the meat will continue to rise by as much as ten degrees when rested, so remove the joint a little before your required temperature.

Start roasting at 220°C/Fan 200°C/Gas 7 for the first 20 minutes to seal the meat and then lower the temperature to 180°C/Fan 160°C/Gas 4.

	TOTAL ROASTING TIME	INTERNAL TEMP
Rare	20 minutes per 450g (1 lb) plus 20 minutes	70°C
Medium	25 minutes per 450g (1 lb) plus 20 minutes	75°C
Well done	30 minutes per 450g (1 lb) plus 20 minutes	80°C

* For roast rack of lamb see page 59
* For slow-roast shoulder of lamb see *Lamb boulangère* page 60

Tapenade and parsley stuffed roast leg of lamb

SERVES 6

approx 1.8kg (4 lb) leg of lamb, tunnel boned

Tapenade and parsley stuffing

175g (6 oz) black olives, pitted

6 anchovies

a large bunch of fresh flat-leaf parsley

2 fat cloves garlic

1 egg yolk

2 tbsp olive oil

To prepare ahead
The leg can be stuffed up to 2 days ahead. To serve hot, cook and serve immediately. It can be cooked 8 hours ahead and served cold, though. Slice just before serving to keep the pink colour.

To cook in the Aga
Roast on the lowest set of runners in the roasting oven for 12–15 minutes per 450g for rare; 20 minutes per 450g for well done. Turn the leg over, or cover with foil if getting too brown.

Many butchers and supermarkets sell part-boned legs of lamb, and this saves on the cooking time. Note the timings given are for pink lamb; if you like yours well done, increase it to 20 minutes per 450g.

Preheat the oven to 220°C/Fan 200°C/Gas 7.

Ask the butcher to tunnel bone the main leg bone out of the leg of lamb. Otherwise, using a sharp knife scrape along the side of the bone and, once you reach the ball and socket joint, cut through the cartilage and discard the bone. You can leave the knuckle end in the leg to keep the shape.

Measure the tapenade ingredients into a processor and whiz for a few seconds to make a coarse mixture. Season with black pepper.

Push the tapenade into the tunnel in the leg of lamb. Rub the leg with olive oil and season with more black pepper.

Sit the lamb in a roasting tin and roast in the preheated oven for about 20 minutes. Reduce the temperature to 180°C/Fan 160°C/Gas 4 and cook for a further 60 minutes. (Cooking time is 20 minutes per 450g [1 lb] – the total time should include the initial 20 minutes.)

Remove the lamb to a carving board and rest covered for about 15 minutes. Serve with a selection of vegetables and home-made gravy (see page 146–7).

Lancashire hotpot

SERVES 6

750g (1 lb 10 oz) peeled white
    potatoes, thickly sliced

3 large carrots, peeled and sliced

3 large sticks celery, sliced

225g (8 oz) lamb kidneys

700g (1 lb 9 oz) shoulder of lamb,
    cut into 2cm (¾ in) pieces

150ml (¼ pint) white wine

300ml (½ pint) chicken stock

To prepare ahead

Can be made ahead and
reheated on the hob or in a
low oven. Freezes well.

To cook in the Aga

Bring to the boil on the
boiling plate, cover and
transfer to the simmering
oven for about 2½ hours.
Remove lid and slide on the
lowest set of runners in the
roasting oven for about 30
minutes.

---

*This is not exactly like the classic recipe, since I've added more
kidneys than usual and included a drop of wine but this is
how I've cooked it for years. Depending on the size of the dish
you are using, you may need more stock.*

Preheat the oven to 180°C/ Fan 160°C/Gas 4. You will need a deep
casserole with a lid.

Put half of the sliced potatoes to one side and mix the remaining
potatoes with the carrots and celery.

Trim the kidneys, removing any hard pieces in the middle, and cut
each kidney into six.

Put half the mixed vegetables in the base of the casserole dish and
season with salt and pepper. Scatter half of the kidneys and half of the
diced lamb over this and season again. Arrange the remaining mixed
vegetables on top, season and place the final layer of lamb and kidneys
in the casserole and season once more. Cover with the wine and stock.

Arrange the reserved sliced potatoes over the top, so the surface is
covered, press down and season again. Cover with a circle of non-stick
paper and a lid (or foil).

Transfer to the preheated oven for about 2 hours.

After 2 hours, remove the lid and paper, and baste the potatoes with
the cooking liquid. Increase the oven temperature to 200°C/Fan 180°C/
Gas 6 and return to the oven for a further 30 minutes until lightly
brown on top.

Serve piping hot.

Winter lamb hotpot

SERVES 6

25g (1 oz) butter

900g (2 lb) neck fillet of lamb,
    sliced into 2cm (¾ in) pieces

2 large onions, sliced thickly

500g (1 lb 2 oz) carrots, peeled
    and thickly sliced

40g (1½ oz) plain flour

600ml (1 pint) cold chicken stock

1kg (2 lb 4 oz) potatoes, peeled
    and thickly sliced

To prepare ahead
Can be made up to a day
ahead and reheated on the
hob or in a low oven. Freezes
well cooked for up to 2
months.

To cook in the Aga
Once the casserole is covered
with foil, transfer to the
grid shelf on the floor of
the roasting oven for about
30 minutes. Transfer to the
simmering oven for about
2 hours or until the lamb
is tender. Remove the foil
and slide on to the top set of
runners in the roasting oven
for about 15 minutes until the
potatoes are brown.

*This is a classic hotpot that uses scrag end and middle
neck of lamb, which is difficult to get now. My lot prefer
neck fillet and I thicken the stew a little, too.*

Preheat the oven to 160°C/Fan 140°C/Gas 3.

Melt half the butter in a deep frying pan over a high heat. Brown the
lamb on both sides and remove with a slotted spoon to a plate and set
aside.

Add the remaining butter to the pan and melt with the onions and
carrots; fry for about 4 minutes.

Measure the flour into a cup and mix with a little of the measured cold
stock until you have a smooth runny paste.

Add the remaining stock to the pan and pour in the flour paste. Bring
to the boil, stirring until thickened and bubbling.

Return the lamb to the pan and season with salt and pepper. Tip into a
shallow ovenproof dish and arrange the sliced potatoes on top. Season
with salt and pepper.

Cover tightly with foil and transfer to the preheated oven for about 1½
hours, or until the lamb is tender. Remove the foil, increase the oven
temperature to 220°C/Fan 200°C/Gas 7, and return to the oven for
about 20 minutes to brown the potatoes.

Serve hot with a green vegetable.

French trimmed roast rack of lamb with rich gravy

A quick roast and it looks impressive, too. Buy French-trimmed racks where the chine bone has been removed. In the summer, add some fresh chopped mint to the sauce, if liked.

SERVES 6–8

½ bottle red wine

2 x French trimmed racks lamb
(6 or 7 chops in each)

Gravy

1 onion, chopped

1 carrot, peeled and diced

600ml (1 pint) good meat stock

a dash Worcestershire sauce

1 level tbsp redcurrant jelly

2 tsp soft butter

2 tsp flour

To prepare ahead
The sauce can be made up
to 2 days ahead, adding any
lamb juices at the end. Not
suitable for freezing.

To cook in the Aga
Roast the lamb on the second
set of runners in the roasting
oven for 15–20 minutes.

Preheat the oven to 220°C/Fan 200°C/Gas 7.

Measure the red wine into a wide-based pan and boil over a high heat until it has reduced to 100ml (3½ fl oz). Set aside.

Trim the skin from the racks and score the fat using a sharp knife. Season.

Heat a large frying pan and put the racks fat side down in the pan. Brown for about 5 minutes, or until dark golden brown. Transfer to a roasting tin, browned side up and bones facing the centre.

Roast in the preheated oven for 25–30 minutes.

Cover the racks with foil and rest for 5 minutes.

Meanwhile, to make the gravy, add the onion and carrot to the unwashed frying pan. Fry for about 5 minutes over a high heat until golden.

Add the reduced wine and stock and boil for about 5 minutes until reduced to about 450ml (16 fl oz). Stir in the Worcestershire sauce and redcurrant jelly. Strain through a sieve into a saucepan.

Measure the butter and flour into a bowl and mix to combine. Add half to the hot sauce and quickly whisk over a high heat until blended. Add the remaining flour and butter paste and whisk again. Bring to the boil to thicken and season with salt and pepper.

Carve the lamb in between the chops and serve with the rich gravy.

Lamb boulangère

SERVES 6

1.5kg (3 lb 5 oz) whole shoulder
    of lamb

3 cloves garlic, sliced

2 large onions, thickly sliced

1kg (2 lb 4 oz) large potatoes,
    peeled and thickly sliced

a bunch of fresh thyme

850ml (1½ pints) chicken stock

To prepare ahead
Arranging the vegetables and
first roasting can be done up
to 6 hours ahead. Slow roast
in a low oven and then serve.

To cook in the Aga
Roast the first part in the
roasting oven for 30 minutes
and then place in the
simmering oven for about 5–6
hours.

*A classic slow-roast shoulder of lamb recipe and one I love to
do for all the family on a Sunday. It is an all-in-one dish, easy
to carve and serve.*

Preheat the oven to 220°C/Fan 200°C/Gas 7.

With a sharp knife make cuts in the shoulder of lamb on the top side.
Stuff the holes with the garlic slices and season the joint with salt and
pepper.

Scatter half the onions in a roasting tin or a 2.4 litre (4 pint) shallow
ovenproof dish and arrange half of the potatoes on top. Arrange half
the thyme on top of this and pour over half the stock. Season with salt
and pepper. Repeat the layers using the remaining onions, potatoes,
thyme and stock.

Sit the lamb on top of the vegetables and roast in the preheated oven for
about 30–40 minutes, or until the lamb is brown. Cover the whole dish
(including the lamb) with foil and reduce the temperature to 140°C/
Fan 120°C/Gas 2. Return to the oven and slow cook for 4–5 hours, or
until the lamb and vegetables are tender. Baste them halfway through
the cooking time.

Carve and serve with the onions and potatoes and an extra green
vegetable.

Oxford meatballs with pepper sauce

SERVES 6

2 tbsp olive oil

2 large onions, finely chopped

450g (1 lb) minced lamb

3 tbsp chopped fresh parsley

150g (5½ oz) Oxford blue cheese, coarsely grated

1 egg yolk

100g (4 oz) breadcrumbs

2 tbsp lemon juice

Pepper sauce

2 cloves garlic

2 red peppers, diced

25g (1 oz) flour

200ml (⅓ pint) apple juice

300ml (½ pint) beef stock

To prepare ahead
The sauce and meatballs can be made up to a day ahead but keep them separate. Both freeze well. Heat the sauce in a pan and then add the meatballs to cook.

To cook in the Aga
Soften the onions in the simmering oven for about 20 minutes. Cook the meatballs and sauce on the boiling plate, cover and transfer to the simmering oven for 30–35 minutes, or until cooked.

These are wonderfully flavoured with Oxford blue cheese. If the cheese is a little too soft to grate, pop it in the freezer for about 20 minutes – this will make the process easier.

Heat 1 tablespoon oil in a shallow pan or casserole, add the onions and fry for a couple of minutes over a high heat. Lower the heat, cover with a lid and cook for about 20 minutes, or until soft. Leave to cool.

To make the meatballs, spoon half of the cold onions into a large mixing bowl. Add the minced lamb, parsley, cheese, egg yolk, breadcrumbs and lemon juice, and season with salt and pepper. Using your hands mix together until combined evenly (the mixture should be fairly wet). Shape into 30 balls.

Heat 1 tablespoon oil in a large frying pan and fry the meatballs over a high heat until golden. Drain on kitchen paper.

Add the garlic and peppers to the pan and stir in the remaining cooked onions. Fry over a high heat for 2 minutes.

Measure the flour into a bowl and stir in half the apple juice to make a smooth mixture.

Pour the stock into the frying pan and stir. Add the flour mixture and the remaining apple juice and bring to the boil, stirring continuously.

Finally, add the meatballs to the pan, cover with a lid, and gently simmer over a low heat for about 25–30 minutes, stirring occasionally until the meatballs are cooked through. If some of the liquid has evaporated, add a little more stock.

Serve with egg noodles.

Braised lamb shanks with apple and caper sauce

SERVES 6

6 small lamb shanks

75g (3 oz) butter

3 large onions, roughly chopped

6 large sticks celery, sliced

40g (1½ oz) flour

300ml (½ pint) apple juice

150ml (¼ pint) chicken stock

2–3 tbsp double cream

3 tbsp capers, drained

To prepare ahead
This can be made completely
up to 2 days ahead and
reheated on the hob or in
a moderate oven to serve.
Freezes well.

To cook in the Aga
Fry on the boiling plate, cover
and transfer to the simmering
oven for about 2½–3 hours,
or until tender.

*If you find that a whole lamb shank is too much for some,
you can just divide a couple in two and remove the bones
before serving.*

Preheat the oven to 160°C/Fan 140°C/Gas 3.

Heat a large flameproof casserole over a high heat, add the shanks
and brown on all sides until dark brown – you will need to do this in
batches. Lift out on to a plate and put to one side.

Add the butter to the pan, and then add the onions and celery and fry
for 5 minutes over a high heat until beginning to soften.

Measure the flour into a bowl, stir in half the apple juice and mix to a
smooth paste.

Add the remaining apple juice and the stock to the frying pan and
bring to the boil. Pour a little of this liquid on to the blended flour and
apple juice. Stir well and then add it to the pan. Cook over a medium
heat, stirring until thickened.

Return the lamb to the pan and season with salt and pepper. Bring to
the boil, cover with a lid and transfer to the preheated oven for about
2–2 ½ hours, or until the meat is tender and falling off the bone.

Stir in the cream and capers and serve piping hot.

Pepperpot tomato and pesto lamb

SERVES 6

2 red peppers

1 tbsp oil

1kg (2 lb 4 oz) lean shoulder of
    lamb, cut into 2.5cm (1 in)
    cubes

2 large onions, sliced

3 cloves garlic, crushed

2 tbsp flour

2 x 400g can chopped tomatoes

150ml (¼ pint) beef or chicken
    stock

1–2 tbsp redcurrant jelly

2 tbsp basil pesto (fresh or from
    a jar)

To prepare ahead
This can be made completely
up to a day ahead. Reheat
gently to serve. Stir in the
pesto just before serving.
Freezes well cooked for up to
2 months.

To cook in the Aga
Roast the peppers on a baking
sheet on the top set of runners
in the roasting oven. Start
the casserole on the boiling
plate. After adding the lamb
and chopped peppers, cover
and transfer to the simmering
oven for about 2 hours.

*Usually casseroles are for winter lunches but this one is good
for summer served with a green salad and rice.*

Preheat the oven to 160°C/Fan 140°C/Gas 3.

Cut the peppers in half and remove the seeds and any white pith. Sit
them on a baking sheet, cut side down and slide under a hot grill until
the skin has blackened. While still hot, put them into a plastic bag and
seal the top until the peppers are cold. Remove the skin and chop the
flesh finely.

Meanwhile, heat the oil in a flameproof casserole over a high heat and
brown the lamb until golden on each side (you may need to do this in
batches). Transfer to a plate.

Add the onions and garlic to the casserole and fry for a minute. Lower
the temperature on the hob, cover and cook for about 5 minutes.

Sprinkle in the flour and fry for a further minute. Add the tomatoes,
stock and redcurrant jelly, and season with salt and pepper.

Return the lamb to the pan and add the chopped peppers. Bring to the
boil, stirring, cover and transfer to the preheated oven for about 1½–2
hours, or until the lamb is tender.

Stir in the pesto, check seasoning and serve hot with rice or mashed
potato.

Pork

Pork roasting chart

Roast pork with golden, crispy, crunchy crackling is a must. Ask your butcher to score the skin very finely with a Stanley knife. Rub the top surface of the crackling with oil and smear with salt and then roast as below. Loin of pork is our favoured cut and gives wonderful crackling.

If you find carving the crackling a problem – lift the skin off the joint before roasting by sliding a sharp knife between the fat and the skin, and then roast the crackling alongside the joint in a small roasting tin, lined with foil for easy cleaning. You can then snip the crackling into pieces with scissors and serve with the carved joint. (If you are cooking the crackling separately like this, make sure you season the joint with salt and pepper.)

The timings given below are a guide, depending on the size of your joint. Bear in mind that a thicker joint weighing the same amount as a longer, thinner joint will take a bit more time to roast. Also, ovens vary a lot in efficiency and thermostats are not always accurate. Using a meat thermometer will eliminate the guesswork, but make sure the thermometer is not touching a bone when you test the meat. The internal temperature of the meat will continue to rise by as much as ten degrees when rested, so remove the joint a little before your required temperature.

Start roasting at 220°C/Fan 200°C/Gas 7 and then after 30 minutes reduce the temperature to 180°C/Fan 160°C/Gas 4.

	TOTAL ROASTING TIME	INTERNAL TEMP
Medium	25 minutes per 450g (1 lb) plus 20 minutes	75°C
Well done	30 minutes per 450g (1 lb) plus 20 minutes	80°C

* For pork fillet see page 69
* For slow-roast shoulder of pork see timings for lamb shoulder on page 60

Honey spiced pork casserole

SERVES 6

100g (4 oz) ready-to-eat dried apricots

600ml (1 pint) good chicken or beef stock

2 cloves garlic

3 tbsp oil

750g (1 lb 10 oz) pork shoulder, cut into 2.5cm (1 in) cubes

2 tbsp runny honey

1 large onion, coarsely sliced

1 medium leek, coarsely sliced

2 small sticks celery, coarsely sliced

1 tsp cumin powder

1 tsp mixed spice

2 tsp ginger powder

50g (2 oz) pistachio nuts, shelled

1 tbsp chopped fresh coriander or parsley

> **To prepare ahead**
> Can be made up to 2 days ahead and reheated on the hob or in a low oven. Freezes well.
>
> **To cook in the Aga**
> Bring to the boil on the boiling plate, cover and transfer to the simmering oven for about 2 hours or until tender.

This is a pork casserole with an intense flavour of spices and natural sweetness. If you are allergic to nuts just omit them.

Preheat the oven to 160°C/Fan 140°C/Gas 3.

Measure the apricots into a heatproof bowl. Heat the stock until just boiling and pour over the apricots. Set aside for about 30 minutes to plump up.

Place the apricots and half the stock (reserve the remainder) in a processor. Add the garlic and whiz until smooth. Tip into a bowl.

Heat 1 tablespoon oil in a large flameproof casserole and add the pork. Pour over the honey and fry over a high heat until golden brown all over (you may need to do this in batches). Remove the pork and set aside.

Add the remaining oil, the onion, leek and celery and fry for a few minutes over a high heat. Sprinkle in the cumin, mixed spice and ginger and fry again. Add the apricot purée, reserved stock and the nuts. Season with salt and pepper, return the pork to the pan and bring to the boil.

Cover and transfer to the preheated oven or simmer on the hob for about 1½–2 hours, or until tender.

Check the seasoning and garnish with coriander or parsley and serve immediately with rice or mash and a green vegetable.

Roast fillets of pork with prune and apple

a knob of butter

1 large onion, roughly chopped

1 medium Bramley apple, peeled and chopped very finely

3 good pork sausages, skinned

50g (2 oz) ready-to-eat dried prunes, roughly chopped

1 tbsp fresh sage, chopped

2 x 450g (1 lb) pork fillets, trimmed

8 slices Parma ham

Gravy

1 tablespoon flour

150ml (¼ pint) apple juice

150ml (¼ pint) stock

To prepare ahead
Can be stuffed and kept raw in the fridge up to a day ahead. Freezes well stuffed and raw.

To cook in the Aga
Roast on the second set of runners in the roasting oven for about 50 minutes.

A wonderful roast – using the tender fillet and served with a fruit stuffing.

Preheat the oven to 220°C/Fan 200°C/Gas 7.

First make the stuffing – melt the butter in a frying pan over a high heat, add the onion and fry for a minute. Cover and cook over a low heat for about 15 minutes or until tender. Add the apple and toss for a few moments. Set aside to cool.

Put the sausagemeat, prunes and sage in a bowl, season with salt and pepper, and then tip in the onion and apple. Stir to combine.

Arrange the two fillets on a board, cover with cling film and, using a rolling pin, bash them so they are about a third thinner but equal in size.

Remove the cling film, spread the stuffing over one fillet and sit the other fillet on top.

Lay four slices of Parma ham on a board, slightly overlapping and sit the fillets on top so they lie across the ham. Roll up like a roulade so the Parma ham is sealed underneath.

Sit in a roasting tin and roast in the preheated oven for about 45–55 minutes until crispy and cooked though. Transfer to a plate to rest.

To make the gravy, sprinkle the flour into the roasting tin, place over a high heat and whisk in the apple juice and stock. Serve with slices of the stuffed pork.

Parmesan and herb frikadellers

SERVES 6

250g (9 oz) minced pork

250g (9 oz) minced beef

50g (2 oz) fresh breadcrumbs

100g (4 oz) Parmesan cheese, finely grated

1 tbsp Dijon mustard

1 heaped tbsp fresh thyme leaves, chopped

1 heaped tbsp chopped fresh sage leaves

1 egg yolk

Roasted red pepper sauce

3 red peppers

2 tbsp oil

1 large onion, roughly chopped

1 x 400g can chopped tomatoes

1 tbsp balsamic vinegar

2 tsp brown sugar

a dash of Tabasco

To prepare ahead
The sauce and frikadellers can be made up to 2 days ahead. Both freeze well.

To cook in the Aga
Roast the peppers on a baking sheet on the top set of runners in the roasting oven for 25 minutes. Bring the sauce to the boil, add the frikadellers and transfer to the simmering oven for 30–40 minutes.

These delicious oval meatballs are full of flavour and served with a lightly spiced sauce.

Preheat the oven to 220°C/Fan 200°C/Gas 7.

First make the red pepper sauce. Slice each pepper in half through the stem and remove the seeds and stalk. Place them cut side down on a baking sheet and drizzle with a little oil. Roast in the preheated oven for about 30 minutes, or until the skins are nearly black. Transfer to a plastic bag and seal the top. Leave to cool. Once cold, peel off the skin and discard.

Pour the remaining oil into a frying pan. Add the onion and fry over a high heat for a minute. Lower the heat, cover and simmer for about 15 minutes or until the onion is soft.

Tip the onion into a processor. Add the peppers, tomatoes, vinegar, sugar and Tabasco and whiz until smooth. Pour into a shallow, wide-based saucepan and season with salt and pepper.

Reduce the oven temperature to 180°C/Fan 160°C/Gas 4.

To make the frikadellers, measure all the remaining ingredients into a bowl. Season with salt and pepper and mix, using your hands, until combined. Divide into 24 and then shape each one into an oval.

Heat the sauce on the hob in a large flameproof casserole or frying pan, add the frikadellers in a single layer, cover with a lid and bring to the boil. Transfer to the oven for about 25 minutes, or until cooked through.

Serve piping hot with rice or egg noodles.

Pork stroganoff

SERVES 6

750g (1 lb 10 oz) pork fillet, sliced
into thin strips

1 tsp honey

2 tbsp oil

a knob of butter

2 large onions, thinly sliced

250g (9 oz) chestnut mushrooms,
thickly sliced

2 tsp paprika

2 level tbsp flour

100ml (3½ fl oz) sherry

200ml (⅓ pint) full-fat crème
fraîche

the juice of ½ lemon

To prepare ahead
The pork can be browned up
to 6 hours ahead. Continue as
detailed (right) and serve. Not
suitable for freezing.

To cook in the Aga
Cook the onions in the
simmering oven for about
20 minutes. Continue on the
boiling plate.

*This is very quick to do and tastes just divine. Pork fillet is
quick to cook, unlike some other cuts of pork.*

Toss the pork strips in the honey and season with salt and pepper.

Pour the oil into a large frying and fry the pork quickly over a high heat
until brown all over. Transfer to a plate.

Melt the butter in the pan, add the onions and fry over a high heat for
a couple of minutes. Cover, lower the heat and simmer for about 20
minutes, or until soft.

Turn up the heat, add the mushrooms and fry for a couple of minutes.
Sprinkle in the paprika and flour and fry for another minute. Add the
sherry and crème fraîche and bring to the boil, stirring, and allow to
thicken. Season with salt and pepper.

Return the pork to the pan, add the lemon juice and heat through for 2
minutes.

Serve hot with rice.

Chicken

Chicken roasting chart

Always buy the best-quality chicken that you can afford. The tastiest are free-range birds that have been well fed. If you wish to stuff the bird, only stuff the neck cavity because the centre of the bird is the last to be penetrated by heat and, therefore, is not safe to fill with stuffing. I much prefer to cook any stuffing in an open dish, though, so that it is crispy and easy to serve. It is traditional to truss the bird with string so that it keeps its shape, but I find this a bother and prefer just to tuck the wings under the body and put herb flavourings, such as rosemary and bay, in the body cavity with some lemon peelings or empty lemon shells, and a few pieces of onion and garlic cloves. Any juice in the tin can be used for gravy once the bird has roasted.

To roast the chicken, season lightly and smear the breast and legs with butter. If the breast is getting too brown during roasting, cover loosely with foil. To test for doneness, insert a skewer into the thickest part of the thigh close to the body of the bird. When it is done the juices that flow out will be clear; if they are still pink, roast a little longer. Baste the bird with its juices from time to time and rest the chicken before carving and while making the gravy.

TIME
20 minutes per 500g (1 lb 2 oz) plus 20 minutes

TEMPERATURE
200°C/Fan 180°/Gas 6

Turkey roasting chart

I use a meat thermometer when cooking turkey as it helps to judge when the turkey is done. Cook it to an internal temperature of 75–80°C, rather than the 90°C suggested on the thermometer gauge, though. When working out when to put the turkey in the oven, allow for at least 30 minutes' resting time.

Loosen the skin over the breast of the turkey by slipping your fingers between the flesh and the skin at the neck, leaving the skin attached at the cavity end. Holding the skin up, spread softened butter over the top of the breast under the skin. Slip in some lemon slices and thyme. (This is a nice addition but, if time is short, you can leave it out.) Stuff the neck end of the turkey up to the breast with the stuffing. Secure the loose skin with fine skewers or just tuck the skin underneath. Fill the body cavity with any lemon trimmings or shells, herbs and large pieces of onion. Tie the legs with string to give a neat shape and lightly butter the skin. Arrange two large sheets of foil across a large roasting tin – enough to go generously over the turkey breast. Place the turkey on top and, if using a meat thermometer, insert into the thickest part of the thigh. Fold the sheets of foil loosely over the turkey, leaving a large air gap between the turkey and the foil.

Calculate the cooking time using the chart below. (There is no need to include the weight of the stuffing.) Roast according to your calculations and then take the turkey out of the oven, turn back the foil and drain off any surplus juices from the tin into a jug or bowl. Baste the bird and then return the turkey to the hot oven to brown and crisp for about 30 minutes. Meanwhile, leave the fat to rise to the top of the jug or bowl in a cold place. When the liquid is cold, take off the fat with a spoon and save any juices for the gravy.

Take the turkey out of the oven and check to see if it is cooked. If you are not using a thermometer, pierce the thickest part of the thigh with a small, sharp knife. If the juices run clear, then the turkey is done; if they are still tinged with pink, then roast for a little longer. If the turkey is already brown enough, though, cover again with the foil. Once cooked, cover the turkey and leave to rest for 30 minutes before carving.

Start roasting at 220°C/Fan 200°C/Gas 7 and then after 30 minutes reduce the temperature to 160°C/Fan 140°C/Gas 3 and then roast according to the times below. Finally, increase the temperature to 220°C/Fan 200°C/Gas 7 for an additional 30 minutes browning time.

WEIGHT	SERVES	THAWING TIME	APPROX ROASTING TIME AT 160°C/FAN 140°C/GAS 3
3.5–5kg (8–11 lb)	8–10	18–20 hours	2 hours 30 minutes – 3 hours 30 minutes
5.4–6.3kg (12–14 lb)	12–15	20–24 hours	3 hours – 4 hours
6.75–9kg (15–20 lb)	15–20	24–30 hours	4 hours – 5 hours

Orange and honey marinated roast chicken

SERVES 6

1.5 kg (3 lb 5 oz) fresh whole
    chicken

25g (1 oz) butter

25g (1 oz) plain flour

Marinade

600ml (1 pint) orange juice from
    a carton

3 cloves garlic, crushed

3 tbsp soy sauce

4 tbsp runny honey

1 large tbsp fresh thyme leaves,
    chopped

To prepare ahead

The chicken can be marinated
up to a day ahead. Freezes well
raw in the marinade.

To cook in the Aga

Roast in the roasting oven for
about an hour, or until cooked.

I have used a similar marinade over the years for lamb, duck legs and poussin, as it is one of my favourite combinations of flavours. I think it is equally good here with roast chicken. There is no last minute gravy to make, as the marinade makes plenty of gravy.

Measure the marinade ingredients into a jug and stir until combined.

Take two large poly bags and put one inside the other. Put the chicken inside the bags and pour over the marinade. Securely tightly and leave to marinate in the fridge overnight.

Preheat the oven to 200°C/Fan 180°C/Gas 6.

Remove the chicken from the marinade and sit in a roasting tin. Roast in the preheated oven for about 1 hour 30 minutes (20 minutes per 450g [1 lb] and 20 minutes over). During the final 15 minutes of cooking, remove any fat from the bottom of the tin and pour the marinade over the chicken. Return to the oven and continue to roast until the chicken is tender. If it starts getting too brown, cover with a piece of foil.

Mix the butter and flour together in a small bowl to make a paste (this is called beurre manié).

Remove the chicken from the roasting tin and set aside to rest. Slide the tin over a high heat on the hob and, using a small hand whisk, add small amounts of beurre manié and whisk to thicken the sauce.

Strain the sauce and serve with the carved chicken.

Chicken fricassée with butternut squash

SERVES 4

4 large chicken legs

900ml (1½ pints) chicken stock

250g (9 oz) butternut squash, peeled, seeded and cut into 2cm (¾ in) cubes

200g (7 oz) potatoes, peeled and cut into 2cm (¾ in) cubes

200g (7 oz) frozen broad beans

40g (1½ oz) plain flour

2 tbsp chopped fresh parsley

To prepare ahead
The casserole can be made completely up to a day ahead and reheated on the hob or in a low oven. Freezes well.

To cook in the Aga
Bring the stock and chicken legs to the boil on the boiling plate, cover and transfer to the simmering oven for about 40 minutes, or until tender. Continue on the boiling plate.

This is a comforting casserole, complete in one dish and cooked on the hob. Use a medium whole chicken, rather than legs, if you prefer.

Arrange the chicken legs in a large flameproof casserole, just large enough to take the legs. Cover with the chicken stock. Bring to the boil, cover and simmer on the hob for about 35 minutes until the legs are tender.

Remove the chicken legs, discard the skin and bone, and slice the meat into large pieces.

Add the squash and potatoes to the hot stock in the pan. Bring to the boil and simmer for about 8–10 minutes. Add the broad beans and continue to simmer for another 5 minutes until all the vegetables are tender.

Measure the flour into a small bowl and mix with a little cold water to make a smooth paste. Add 3 tablespoons of the hot stock to the flour bowl and mix until smooth. Pour the flour paste into the casserole dish and stir over a high heat until the sauce has thickened.

Season with salt and pepper, add the chicken and parsley to the pan and serve piping hot.

Oriental chicken with water chestnuts

SERVES 6

4 large chicken breasts, skinned
and sliced into 3 thick slices

1 tbsp oil

1 x 275g can water chestnuts,
thinly sliced

1 tbsp cornflour

250g (9 oz) small chestnut
mushrooms, halved

300ml (½ pint) cold chicken
stock

4 tbsp full-fat crème fraîche

2 tbsp chopped fresh coriander

Marinade

1 tbsp runny honey

2 cloves garlic, crushed

1 tsp fresh ginger, grated

3 tbsp soy sauce

3 tbsp hoi-sin sauce

To prepare ahead
Can be assembled completely
up to 8 hours ahead and baked
as detailed (right) to serve.
Freezes well.

To cook in the Aga
Bake the dish on the second
set of runners in the roasting
oven for 15 minutes.

*An all-in-one-dish recipe – perfect for making ahead. With
its oriental marinade, this gives a lovely change to the classic
roast.*

Preheat the oven to 200°C/Fan 180°C/Gas 6.

To make the marinade, measure the honey, garlic, ginger, soy and hoi-sin sauce into a bowl and whisk by hand to combine. Add the strips of chicken and stir to coat in the sauce. Cover, transfer to the fridge and marinate for a minimum of 3 hours.

Heat the oil in a large frying pan. Remove the chicken from the marinade (reserve it for the sauce) and brown the chicken very quickly over a high heat so it is golden on all sides. Spoon the chicken into a single layer in an ovenproof dish and scatter over the sliced water chestnuts.

Measure the cornflour into a bowl and add 2 tablespoons of cold water and mix to a smooth paste.

Wipe the frying pan with a piece of damp kitchen paper to remove any dark marinade. Add the mushrooms and fry for a few minutes over a high heat. Add the reserved marinade, the chicken stock and crème fraîche and bring to the boil, stirring continuously. Stir in the cornflour mixture, check the seasoning and bring to the boil to thicken. Pour over the chicken.

Bake in the preheated oven for about 10–15 minutes, or until the chicken is cooked through and the sauce is bubbling. Sprinkle with coriander and serve hot.

Coq au vin

SERVES 6

25g (1 oz) dried porcini
    mushrooms

1 x bottle red wine

50g (2 oz) butter

6 chicken leg joints

200g (7 oz) bacon lardons or
    chopped streaky bacon

500g (1 lb 2 oz) pickling onions,
    peeled

400g (14 oz) small button
    mushrooms, left whole

40g (1½ oz) plain flour

2 cloves garlic, sliced

6 sprigs of thyme

3 tbsp tomato purée

2 tbsp redcurrant jelly

To prepare ahead
Can be made up to 2 days
ahead and reheated on the hob
or in a low oven. Freezes well
cooked.

To cook in the Aga
Bring to the boil on the boiling
plate, cover and transfer to the
simmering oven for an hour,
or until the chicken is tender.

A classic recipe full of flavour and punch.

Preheat the oven to 180°C/ Fan 160°C/Gas 4.

Soak the porcini mushrooms in 300ml (½ pint) boiling water for 15
minutes.

Pour the wine into a saucepan. Add the porcini mushrooms and their
liquid. Bring up to the boil and then boil over a high heat until it has
reduced to about 600ml (1 pint).

Melt half the butter in a large flameproof casserole over a high heat. Fry
the chicken legs until golden brown and crispy (you may need to do this
in batches). Transfer to a plate.

Add the remaining butter and fry the bacon and onions for 5 minutes
until starting to turn golden. Transfer to a plate.

Add the button mushrooms and fry for 3–4 minutes. Return the onions
and bacon to the pan.

Mix the flour in a jug with 3 tablespoons of cold water to make a thin
paste. Add the reduced wine and porcini mushrooms and mix together
until smooth. Add this liquid to the pan and stir over the heat until it has
thickened (it will be very thick at this point).

Stir in the garlic, thyme, tomato purée and redcurrant jelly, and return the
chicken legs to the pan, gently pushing down into the sauce. Season with
salt and pepper and bring to the boil. Cover with a lid and transfer to the
preheated oven for about 40–45 minutes until the chicken is tender.

Check the seasoning and serve with mashed potatoes and vegetables.

Peppadew pepper chicken

1 x 375g jar mild peppadew
    peppers

2 tbsp oil

2 medium onions, thinly sliced

2 cloves garlic, crushed

3 level tbsp flour

150ml (¼ pint) cold chicken
    stock

2 x 400g can chopped tomatoes

2 tbsp tomato purée

2 tbsp brown sugar

12 chicken thighs, skinned but
    bone in

2 tbsp chopped fresh parsley

To prepare ahead
Can be made up to a day
ahead and reheated on the hob
or in a low oven. Freezes well
cooked for up to 2 months. If a
little thick when reheating add
a touch more stock.

To cook in the Aga
Bring to the boil on the boiling
plate, cover with a lid and
transfer to the simmering oven
for about 1½ hours, or until
tender.

*A very simple chicken casserole, as the thighs are not browned
ahead. The sauce is spicy and flecked with the peppadew
pepper. If you wish to use chicken thighs without the bone, it
will only take about 45 minutes to cook.*

Preheat the oven to 180°C/Fan 160°C/Gas 4.

Measure 15 peppadew peppers into a processor or blender and whiz until
chopped very finely.

Heat the oil in a large flameproof casserole. Add the onions and fry over a
high heat for about 5 minutes until starting to soften. Add the garlic and
fry for a further minute.

Measure the flour into a small bowl and mix with a third of the chicken
stock and all the tomatoes to give a smooth paste.

Add the remaining stock, tomato purée, sugar, whizzed peppadew and
the flour paste to the frying pan. Stir and bring to the boil.

Add 3 tablespoons of the peppadew juice from the jar and the chicken
thighs, and season with salt and pepper. Stir and bring back to the boil.
Cover with a lid and transfer to the preheated oven for 1–1½ hours until
the chicken thighs are tender.

Check seasoning before sprinkling with parsley and serving with rice.

Lemon chicken with chives

SERVES 4

25g (1 oz) butter

8 chicken thighs, skinned, bone in

1 large onion, roughly chopped

25g (1 oz) flour

300ml (½ pint) hot chicken stock

finely grated rind and juice of 2 lemons

4 tbsp full-fat crème fraîche

3 tbsp snipped fresh chives

To prepare ahead
Can be made up to a day ahead and reheated on the hob – add the crème fraîche and chives when reheating. Freezes well.

To cook in the Aga
Bring to the boil, cover and transfer to the simmering oven for 45 minutes.

This is a light chicken casserole – I used to make this with chicken joints but I find most people enjoy thighs just as much. If you prefer to remove the bone before cooking, the cooking time should be reduced by 10 minutes.

Melt the butter in a large frying pan over a high heat, add the thighs and brown all over until golden. Season with salt and pepper and then remove with a slotted spoon and set aside.

Add the onion to the pan and fry for 3 minutes. Sprinkle in the flour, add the hot stock and bring to the boil, stirring all the time.

Add the rind and juice of the lemons, and return the thighs to the pan. Season again and bring to the boil. Cover and simmer over a low heat for about 35–45 minutes, or until the thighs are tender.

Stir in the crème fraîche and nearly all the chives.

Serve with mashed potato or rice and sprinkle over the remaining chives.

Tarragon chicken casserole

SERVES 6

2 medium onions, sliced

3 small carrots, peeled and sliced

700ml (1¼ pints) chicken stock

150ml (¼ pint) white wine

juice of ½ lemon

1 x 1.25kg (2 lb 12 oz) chicken

5 sprigs of thyme

25g (1 oz) butter

25g (1 oz) flour

225g (8 oz) chestnut mushrooms, quartered

2–3 tbsp full-fat crème fraîche

a small bunch of fresh tarragon leaves, snipped

To prepare ahead

The casserole can be made completely the day before and gently reheated on the hob – adding the tarragon and crème fraîche just before reheating. Not suitable for freezing.

To cook in the Aga

To cook the chicken, bring the pan to the boil, cover and transfer to the simmering oven for about 2 hours or until the chicken is tender. Continue on the boiling plate.

Choose the best chicken that you can afford. Only make this if you have fresh or frozen tarragon – dried tarragon just isn't good enough.

Place the onions, carrots, stock, wine and lemon juice in a deep saucepan. Put the whole chicken on top and add the lemon shells and thyme sprigs and season. Cover with a lid, bring to the boil and gently simmer for about an hour, or until the chicken is cooked.

Transfer the chicken and vegetables to a bowl and discard the thyme sprigs and lemon shells.

Boil the cooking liquid over a high heat until it has reduced to about 450ml (16 fl oz).

Melt the butter in a saucepan, add the flour and stir over a high heat for a few seconds. Gradually add the reduced liquid, stirring until smooth. Bring to the boil, add the mushrooms and simmer for 2 minutes.

Remove the cooked meat from the chicken carcass and cut into large strips or pieces. Add the chicken and vegetables to the sauce. Stir in the crème fraîche and tarragon, and season with salt and pepper.

Serve hot with rice or mashed potatoes and a green vegetable.

Chicken breasts with white wine and mushrooms

SERVES 4

25g (1 oz) dried porcini
    mushrooms

150ml (¼ pint) white wine

25g (1 oz) butter

6 chicken breasts, skinned

250g (9 oz) small chestnut
    mushrooms, quartered

400ml (14 fl oz) double cream

To prepare ahead
Arrange the cooked cold
chicken breasts in a small
shallow dish that is just large
enough to take the chicken.
Cover with foil and keep in the
fridge with the reduced sauce
in a separate container for up
to 24 hours. To reheat, transfer
the chicken still covered in foil
to a preheated oven 180°C/Fan
160°C/Gas 4 for 20 minutes.
Reheat the sauce and pour
over the top. Not suitable for
freezing.

To cook in the Aga
Soften the mushrooms on
the back of the Aga. Bring the
whole dish to the boil, cover
and transfer to the simmering
oven for about 30 minutes.

This reheats very well so it is a really good prepare-and-cook-ahead recipe. Perfect for a spring lunch. The dried mushrooms add depth to the sauce.

Soak the dried porcini mushrooms in boiling water for at least an hour until soft. Strain, reserving the liquid.

Finely chop the porcini mushrooms and place in a large saucepan over a high heat with the mushroom liquid and the white wine. Bring up to the boil and reduce until you have 150ml (¼ pint).

Heat a frying pan until hot and add half the butter. Season the chicken breasts and brown in the pan on both sides. Set aside.

Add the remaining butter to the pan and fry the chestnut mushrooms for a few minutes. Add the reduced mushroom liquid and the double cream and bring up to the boil.

Return the chicken breasts to the pan, cover with a lid and gently simmer for about 15 minutes until the chicken is cooked through.

Transfer the chicken to a plate to rest for 5 minutes and then carve each breast into four slices.

Check the seasoning and bring the sauce back to the boil and reduce until it has thickened – make sure it is thick enough to coat the back of a spoon.

Serve the chicken with the sauce spooned over the top.

Chicken Miranda

SERVES 6

1 tbsp oil

1 large onion, finely chopped

175g (6 oz) chestnuts, roughly
    chopped

150g (5½ oz) pork sausagemeat

6 chicken breasts, without skin or
    bone

6 long slices streaky bacon

2 tbsp runny honey

Sauce

1 tbsp oil

1 large onion, finely chopped

75ml (2½ fl oz) sherry

250ml (9 fl oz) chicken stock

6 tbsp full-fat crème fraîche

1 tsp cornflour

2 tbsp chopped fresh parsley

To prepare ahead
Chicken breasts can be stuffed
and wrapped in bacon up to
24 hours ahead. Freezes well
raw for up to 2 months. Make
the sauce fresh.

To cook in the Aga
Roast the chicken on the
second set of runners in the
roasting oven for about 25
minutes.

*These are roasted, chestnut-stuffed chicken breasts served in
a light parsley sauce. Use either frozen chestnuts or 75g (3 oz)
dried chestnuts that have been soaked overnight.*

Preheat the oven to 200°C/Fan 180°C/Gas 6 and line a baking sheet with
non-stick baking paper or foil.

First make the stuffing. Heat the oil in a frying pan over a high heat, add
the onion and fry for a minute. Lower the heat, cover and cook for about
10 minutes, or until soft.

Add the chestnuts to the pan and fry over a high heat until lightly toasted.
Spoon the onion and chestnut mixture into a bowl to cool. Once it is cold,
stir in the sausagemeat and season with salt and pepper. Divide into six.

Lay the chicken breasts on a board and slice each breast horizontally
through the middle, leaving it attached on one long side. Spread the
stuffing into the pocket and neatly press the top half back down. Wrap
one slice of bacon around the breast to help keep the filling in place
(make sure the ends of the bacon are underneath).

Sit the breasts on the prepared baking sheet, season them with a little
salt and pepper and drizzle over a touch of honey. Roast in the preheated
oven for 25–30 minutes until golden and cooked through.

Meanwhile, to make the sauce, place the oil in a frying pan over a high
heat. Add the onion and fry for a minute. Lower the heat, cover and cook
for about 10 minutes, or until soft.

Add the sherry and the stock and boil to reduce by half. Stir in the crème
fraîche and any of the chicken juices from the baking sheet.

Measure the cornflour into a bowl and add 2 tablespoons of cold water
and stir until smooth. Pour a quarter of the hot stock and crème fraîche
over the cornflour paste, stir and return to the pan. Stir and boil until
thickened.

Finally, add the parsley to the sauce and serve with the chicken breasts.

Pied Woodpecker

Female Short Eared Owl

Pied Wagtail

Fisher

Female Kestrel

Grebe

Pheasant

Young game birds roasting chart

These timings are for young birds – older game birds are best used in a casserole as the meat can be tougher and therefore needs a longer cooking time. Make sure that the birds have been hung – pheasant should be left for about a week, grouse and partridge for about 3–4 days (although, if the weather is warm, hang for shorter times).

GAME SEASONS

Grouse	12 August – 10 December
Partridge	1 September – 1 February
Pheasant	1 October – 1 February

Before roasting, season the birds, place a little butter, onion and sprigs of fresh thyme into the body cavity and arrange 1 or 2 rashers of streaky bacon over the breast to keep it moist. To test for doneness, the juices should run clear when a skewer is inserted in the thigh. Rest for about 5 minutes before carving.

Start roasting at 220°C/Fan 200°C/Gas 7 and then reduce the temperature to 200°C/Fan 180°C/Gas 6.

	FIRST ROASTING	SECOND ROASTING
Grouse	5 minutes	about 25–35 minutes
Partridge	10 minutes	about 25–30 minutes
Pheasant	10 minutes	about 30–40 minutes

Duck and goose roasting chart

Remove excess fat from the bird's cavity. This can be rendered down by roasting slowly to extract all the fat, which can then be used for roasting potatoes. Any extra can be kept in a jar in the fridge for another occasion.

Stuff the neck end only and fill the body cavity with flavouring, such as lemon, herbs and onion (as for roast chicken). Season the birds and rub a small amount of butter over the breasts and leg. If it is getting too brown during roasting, cover the breast with foil.

TEMPERATURE	TIME
200°C/Fan 180°/Gas 6	15 minutes per 450g (1 lb) plus 15 minutes

• For *Slow-roast duck* see page 94

Young roast pheasant

SERVES 4 – 6

½ small onion, cut in half

a few parsley stalks

a few sprigs of thyme

a brace of young pheasants

50g (2 oz) butter

4 rashers streaky bacon

Gravy

25g (1 oz) butter

1 level tbsp flour

75ml (2½ fl oz) Port

300ml (½ pint) game or chicken
stock

a little redcurrant jelly

a dash of gravy browning

To prepare ahead
Prepare the pheasant and
sit in the tin ready to roast
– roast as detailed (right)
and serve immediately. Not
suitable for freezing.

To cook in the Aga
Roast on the second set of
runners in the roasting oven
for about 35–40 minutes.

*This makes a perfect Sunday lunch. All too often young
pheasants are mucked about with unnecessarily, but a simple
roast pheasant with all the trimmings can be really exciting.
Remember only roast when you are certain the birds are
young; an old bird is guaranteed to be tough and needs long
slow casserole cooking.*

Preheat the oven to 220°C/Fan 200°C/Gas 7.

Place the onion quarters, parsley stalks and thyme sprigs in the cavity
of each bird for flavouring. Smear the breasts of each bird with butter
and dust with black pepper. Cover each breast with 2 rashers of bacon
and sit the birds in a roasting tin. Pour about 2cm (¾ in) of boiling
water into the base of the roasting tin.

Carefully transfer to the preheated oven and roast for 10 minutes.
Reduce the oven temperature to 200°C/Fan 180°C/Gas 6 and roast for
about 30–40 minutes.

Tip the birds so the juices run out of the cavity and into the roasting tin.
Transfer the birds to a plate, cover with foil and keep warm. The birds
will continue to cook while being rested.

To make the gravy, drain any juices from the tin and reserve. Sit the
roasting tin on the hob, add the butter and whisk in the flour. Cook for
a moment. Add the Port, stock, reserved juices and redcurrant jelly, and
bring to the boil, stirring. Strain and add a dash of gravy browning.

Carve the pheasants, serve with the hot gravy and *Fried crumbs*,
Game chips and *Bread sauce* (see pages 100 and 149).

Glazed guinea fowl with lime sauce

1 x 1.125kg (2 lb 8 oz) whole guinea fowl

2 limes

4 tbsp lime marmalade

200ml (⅓ pint) full-fat crème fraîche

To prepare ahead
This is best roasted and served immediately. Not suitable for freezing.

To cook in the Aga
Roast on the lowest set of runners in the roasting oven – first for 25 minutes, then turn it over and roast for a further 30 minutes.

Brushing the guinea fowl with a little lime marmalade gives a dark glaze – keep an eye on the bird while it is roasting, though, and if it's getting too brown cover it with foil.

Preheat the oven to 200°C/Fan 180°C/Gas 6.

Sit the guinea fowl on a small rack in a small roasting tin.

Squeeze the juice from the limes into a bowl and reserve for the sauce. Put the lime shells into the cavity of the bird.

Melt half the marmalade in a small pan. Brush the bird with the marmalade so the breast and legs are completely covered. Season with salt and pepper. Turn the bird upside down in the tin and roast in the preheated oven for 30 minutes.

After 30 minutes, carefully turn the bird the right way up and continue to roast for a further 30–40 minutes, or until cooked through and the juices run clear when a knife is inserted into the thigh. Remove from the tin to a plate and allow to rest.

Remove the grill rack from the tin and add the crème fraîche. With a whisk or spatula mix the crème fraîche into the flavourings from the tin. Pour into a saucepan, add the remaining marmalade and lime juice, and bring to the boil, stirring. Season with salt and pepper and taste the sauce; if it is a little sharp, add a touch more marmalade.

Carve or joint the guinea fowl and serve with the sauce.

Slow-roast duck with orange and Port sauce

SERVES 4

1 duck

2 large oranges

3 level tbsp plain flour

200ml (⅓ pint) game stock

100ml (3½ fl oz) Port

1 tbsp redcurrant jelly

To prepare ahead
The duck is best cooked and served on the day. Not suitable for freezing.

To cook in the Aga
Cook on the lowest set of runners in the roasting oven for about 15 minutes. Transfer to the simmering oven for about 5 hours, or until tender and the meat is falling off the bone. Return to the centre of the roasting oven for about 20 minutes, or until the skin is crisp.

A wonderful way to serve a whole duck. Slow roasting the duck does not dry it out and, with a quick roast at the end, it still has a crispy skin.

Preheat the oven to 140°C/ Fan 120°C/Gas 2.

Place a grill rack in a roasting tin and sit the duck, breast side down, on the rack. Using a small knife remove the skin from the oranges and put into the cavity of the duck.

Roast in the preheated oven for 2½ hours.

Carefully turn the duck over so the breast is on top and return to the oven for a further 2½ hours, giving 5 hours total cooking time.

Increase the heat to 200°C/ Fan 180°C /Gas 6 and roast the duck for 15 minutes to crisp the skin.

Remove the duck from the tin and cover.

To make the sauce, pour the duck fat from the roasting tin into a jug and spoon 3 tablespoons of the fat into a saucepan. Place over a high heat and add the flour. Whisk to combine. Slowly whisk in the stock, Port and any duck juices from the tin (and from the rested joint) and continue to whisk over a high heat until boiling and thickened.

Squeeze the juice from one orange and add to the pan with the redcurrant jelly. Season with salt and pepper, bring back to the boil and simmer for a couple of minutes.

Segment the remaining orange and chop into fine dice. Add to the sauce.

Carve the duck and serve with the hot sauce.

Pheasant casserole with thyme and prunes

SERVES 6

2 whole pheasants

250g (9 oz) smoked bacon
    lardons

2 medium onions, sliced

2 sticks celery, sliced

2 medium carrots, sliced

200ml (⅓ pint) red wine

6 large pitted prunes, chopped

25g (1 oz) plain flour

200ml (⅓ pint) cold game or
    chicken stock

6 sprigs of thyme

about 1 tbsp redcurrant jelly

To prepare ahead
The casserole can be made
up to a day ahead. Reheat the
sauce with the breasts and
legs in a moderate oven and
serve hot. Not suitable for
freezing.

To cook in the Aga
Cover and transfer to the
simmering oven for 2 hours.

The ideal winter recipe. This is a good way of cooking older pheasants, or perhaps pheasants that have been in the freezer for longer than you can remember!

Preheat the oven to 180°C/ Fan 160°C/Gas 4.

Place a large flameproof casserole over a high heat and brown the pheasants on all sides until lightly golden. Remove from the pan and set aside.

Add the bacon to the pan and fry over a high heat until crisp. Add the vegetables and fry for a few more minutes. Add the red wine and prunes and boil for a couple of minutes.

Measure the flour into a bowl and mix with the cold stock until smooth and then pour into the pan. Bring the sauce to the boil, stirring, until thickened.

Add the thyme sprigs and redcurrant jelly and season with salt and pepper. Return the pheasants to the pan, cover and transfer to the preheated oven for about 1 hour.

Remove the pan from the oven and check to see if the breasts are cooked. If so, carve them from the carcasses and then return the carcasses to the pan. Continue to cook the legs for a further 30 minutes, or until tender.

Carve the legs from the carcasses and return them and the breasts to the pan. Heat through for a few minutes until the breasts are piping hot and then serve with the vegetables and sauce.

Duck breasts with cherry sauce

SERVES 6

a knob of soft butter

4 duck breasts, skinned

Cherry sauce

2 tsp cornflour

100ml (3½ fl oz) Port

2 tbsp cherry jam

100ml (3½ fl oz) orange juice

1½ tsp soy sauce

½ tsp balsamic vinegar

To prepare ahead
The sauce can be made up to
a day ahead. The breasts can
be browned up to 8 hours
ahead and then roasted as
detailed (right) to serve (8–9
minutes from cold room
temperature). Not suitable for
freezing.

To cook in the Aga
Fry on the boiling plate and
then roast on the top set of
runners in the roasting oven
for 7 minutes.

A classic recipe but one that everyone loves and perfect for a smart Sunday lunch.

Preheat the oven to 200°C/Fan 180°C/Gas 6.

Spread a little soft butter over each breast and season with salt and pepper.

Place a frying pan over a high heat and brown each breast for 1½ minutes on each side. Immediately transfer to a baking sheet.

Roast in the preheated oven for 7–8 minutes for a pink middle and set aside to rest.

To make the sauce, measure all the ingredients into a pan and whisk until smooth. Bring to the boil and stir until thickened. Season with salt and pepper and any juices from the duck.

Slice each breast into three on the diagonal and serve with the hot sauce.

Spiced venison casserole

SERVES 6

1 tbsp oil

1kg (2 lb 4 oz) braising venison, cut into 4cm (1½ in) cubes

2 large onions, chopped

1 tbsp fresh ginger, peeled and grated

½ tsp ground cumin

½ tsp ground coriander

¼ tsp ground cinnamon

½ tsp turmeric

300ml (½ pint) game, beef or chicken stock

2 tbsp cornflour

1 x 150g tub full-fat Greek yoghurt

juice of ½ lemon

To prepare ahead
Can be made up to 2 days ahead and reheated on the hob or in a low oven. Freezes well cooked.

To cook in the Aga
Bring to the boil on the boiling plate, cover and transfer to the simmering oven for about 2 hours.

This is full of flavour – you can use half beef and half venison, if preferred.

Preheat the oven to 180°C/Fan 160°C/Gas 4.

Put the oil in a large flameproof casserole over a high heat. Add the venison cubes and fry until brown on all sides (you may need to do this in batches). Transfer to a plate.

Add the onions to the pan and fry for 2 minutes. Add the fresh ginger and spices and fry for a couple more minutes. Return the meat to the pan and fry until the mixture is coated in the spices. Add the stock and bring to the boil, stirring.

Measure the cornflour into a bowl and mix with the yoghurt until smooth. Stir into the pan, add the lemon juice and season with salt and pepper. Bring to the boil and stir until thickened. Cover and transfer to the preheated oven for about 1½–2 hours, or until the meat is tender.

Serve hot with winter root vegetables.

Accompaniments for game

Game chips

The correct way to make these is to deep fat fry thin slices of potato. I do not have a deep fat fryer, though, as that method is not my style. I prefer to cheat and buy good quality large plain potato crisps and gently warm them in a very low oven.

Parsley croûtes

2 slices thin bread

1 tbsp finely chopped fresh
    parsley

1 tbsp oil

25g (1 oz) butter

These are very old fashioned but quite attractive!

Cut the crusts from the bread and cut each slice into four triangles.

Sprinkle the parsley on to a small plate.

Place the oil in a frying pan over a high heat, add the butter and melt. Add the bread triangles and fry, turning frequently until they are golden and crisp. Season with salt and pepper.

Carefully remove from the pan and press one side of the triangle into the chopped parsley.

To serve, stand the triangles around the dish or garnish a roast with the parsley ends upright.

Fried crumbs

1 tbsp oil

25g (1 oz) butter

50g (2 oz) fresh white
    breadcrumbs

These are traditional with game and make any game dish extra special.

Place the oil in a frying pan over a medium heat, add the butter and melt.

Tip in the breadcrumbs and fry gently, turning frequently, until the crumbs are pale golden and crisp. Season with salt and pepper and turn into a bowl.

To prepare ahead
They can be made up to two days ahead and reheated in a low oven or the simmering oven of the Aga for about 15 minutes. Freeze well.

Fish

Mushroom and smoked haddock pie

SERVES 6

750g (1 lb 10 oz) potatoes,
    peeled weight

a little hot milk

a knob of butter

6 large eggs

50g (2 oz) mature Cheddar
    cheese, grated

Smoked haddock filling

75g (3 oz) butter, plus an extra
    knob

500g (1 lb 2 oz) button chestnut
    mushrooms, thickly sliced

75g (3 oz) flour

600ml (1 pint) hot milk

150ml (¼ pint) double cream

2 tsp Dijon mustard

750g (1 lb 10 oz) skinned smoked
    haddock, cut into
    large pieces

To prepare ahead
Can be assembled completely
up to 8 hours ahead. Cook
the dish as detailed (right) to
serve. Not suitable for freezing.

To cook in the Aga
Bake on the second set of
runners in the roasting oven
for about 30 minutes.

*A perfect Sunday lunch for all the family and friends, too.
The raw fish cooks in the hot sauce, so there's no need to cook
the fish ahead. If you have hungry teenagers you may want to
increase the potato topping to 1kg (2 lb 4 oz).*

Preheat the oven to 200°C/Fan 180°C/Gas 6. You will need a 2.4 litre
(4 pint) ovenproof dish.

First make the mashed potato. Slice the potatoes into even pieces, tip
them into a saucepan and cover with water and a little salt. Bring to the
boil and, once boiling, cook for 15–20 minutes, or until tender. Drain and
mash the potatoes until smooth with the milk and butter and season with
black pepper.

Meanwhile, put the eggs into a saucepan, cover with cold water, bring to
the boil and cook for 10 minutes. Drain and refresh in cold water. Peel
and slice each egg into quarters.

To make the filling, heat the knob of butter in a deep, wide-based
saucepan. Add the mushrooms and fry over a high heat for a couple of
minutes. Remove with a slotted spoon.

Add the remaining butter to the same unwashed saucepan, tip in the
flour, whisk to a roux and cook for a few moments. Gradually add the
milk, whisking all the time, until boiling and you have a smooth sauce.
Stir in the cream and mustard.

Return the mushrooms to the pan, remove from the heat and add the
haddock and eggs. Season with salt and pepper and stir until combined.

Spoon the filling into the ovenproof dish and spread evenly. Level the top
and cool until firm.

Spoon over the mash and level the top again. Sprinkle with the cheese.

Bake in the preheated oven for about 30–35 minutes until golden and
cooked through.

Stuffed fillets of sole on a bed of spinach

SERVES 4

100g (4 oz) full-fat cream cheese

1 tbsp snipped fresh chives

1 tbsp lemon juice

1 tsp Dijon mustard

4 large lemon sole fillets, skinned

a little melted butter, plus an extra knob

50g (2 oz) Parmesan cheese, grated

a little paprika

1kg (2 lb 4 oz) fresh baby spinach

To prepare ahead
The sole parcels can be made up to a day ahead and kept in the fridge. The spinach can be wilted up to 4 hours ahead and then fried in butter at the last minute. The filled raw sole fillets freeze well.

To cook in the Aga
Cook on the second set of runners in the roasting oven for about 10 minutes.

This recipe is ideal when spinach is in season and you want a delicate lunch. Stuffed sole fillets are full of flavour. A long thin fillet can be difficult to bend and stay in place with the filling inside, so we cut ours halfway through first so it folds easily.

Preheat the oven to 200°C/Fan 180°C/Gas 6 and line a baking sheet with non-stick baking paper.

Measure the cream cheese, chives, lemon juice and Dijon mustard into a bowl. Mix together until combined and season well. Divide the mixture into four.

Lay the sole fillets skinned side up, horizontally on a board. Using a sharp knife, score each fillet in half vertically only half way through the flesh. Turn each fillet over and then spoon a quarter of the chive mixture on to one half of each fillet. Fold the other half over so you have a little parcel with the filling inside. Season well and brush with melted butter.

Place the fillets on the prepared baking sheet and sprinkle them with the cheese and paprika. Cook the sole in the preheated oven for about 12 minutes until cooked through.

While the sole is cooking, heat a large frying pan and add large handfuls of the spinach with a few tablespoons of hot water and toss over a high heat until just wilted. Drain in a colander and squeeze as much water out of the cooked spinach as possible. Repeat until you have wilted all of the spinach. Melt the knob of butter in the frying pan and add the wilted spinach and season well. Toss over a high heat until heated through.

Divide the spinach between four plates. Pile it neatly in the centre of each one and sit a sole parcel on top. Drizzle over any juices and serve.

Salmon and couscous filo tart

SERVES 6

2 tbsp olive oil

1 large onion, chopped

2 red peppers, seeded and cut into 2cm (¾ in) pieces

350g (12 oz) salmon fillet, skin on

75g (3 oz) couscous

150ml (¼ pint) boiling chicken or fish stock

3 tbsp chopped fresh dill

2 tbsp chopped fresh flat-leaf parsley

juice of ½ lemon

3 tbsp green basil pesto

8 sheets filo pastry

25g (1 oz) melted butter

To prepare ahead
Can be made up to 4 hours ahead and reheated in a moderate oven until hot. Not suitable for freezing.

To cook in the Aga
Fry the onion on the boiling plate, cover and transfer to the simmering oven for 20 minutes. Cook the salmon on the lowest set of runners in the roasting oven for 10 minutes. Bake the tart on the grid shelf on the floor of the roasting oven for about 25 minutes.

A lovely change from the more traditional en croûte – make sure the filo is nice and crisp after cooking.

Preheat the oven to 200°C/Fan 180°C/Gas 6 and line a baking sheet with lightly greased foil. You will need a 28cm (11 in) loose-bottomed tart tin.

Heat the oil in a large frying pan. Add the onion and fry over a high heat for about 3 minutes. Lower the heat, cover and cook for about 20 minutes until soft.

Add the peppers and fry for a further 3 minutes.

Sit the salmon, skin side up, on the prepared baking sheet. Cover the top with foil and cook in the preheated oven for about 10 minutes, or until cooked through. Remove the skin and leave to cool.

Measure the couscous into a bowl, pour over the hot stock, stir, cover with cling film and leave for 30 minutes until all the liquid is absorbed. Fluff up with a fork.

Stir the onion and peppers into the couscous. Break the salmon into large flakes and add to the bowl with the dill, parsley, lemon and pesto. Season with salt and pepper and carefully stir to combine.

Brush 5 sheets of filo with melted butter and line the loose-bottomed tin with the pastry so it covers the base and goes up the sides. Spoon the couscous mixture into the tin. Brush the remaining sheets of filo with butter and arrange over the top, so the filling is covered.

Bake in the preheated oven for 25–30 minutes, or until golden brown and crispy.

Cut into wedges and serve with a dressed green salad.

Salmon and spinach bake

SERVES 6

1kg (2 lb 4 oz) frozen whole leaf
  spinach, defrosted

a large knob of butter

4 large eggs

600g (1 lb 5 oz) salmon fillet,
  skinned

500ml (18 fl oz) full-fat crème
  fraîche

100g (4 oz) Parmesan cheese,
  grated

2 level tbsp cornflour

juice of ½ lemon

50g (2 oz) breadcrumbs

To prepare ahead
Can be assembled up to a
day ahead – just add the
breadcrumbs and remaining
cheese before baking as
detailed (right). Not suitable
for freezing.

To cook in the Aga
Bake on the second set of
runners in the roasting oven
for about 35 minutes until
piping hot.

*A complete meal in one dish – whole fillets and a delicious,
creamy, spinach base.*

Preheat the oven to 220°C/Fan 200°C/Gas 7. You will need a wide-based
1.7 litre (3 pint) ovenproof dish.

Drain the spinach and squeeze out as much liquid as you can.

Melt the butter in a frying pan. Add the spinach to the pan and fry in the
butter over a high heat for a few minutes. Season with salt and pepper
and spoon into the base of the dish.

Put the eggs in a pan, cover with cold water, bring to the boil and boil for
10 minutes. Drain and refresh in cold water. Peel and slice each egg into 6.

Cut the salmon into pieces roughly the same size as the egg. Lay the
salmon pieces on top of the spinach in a single layer. Scatter over the eggs
and season.

Add the crème fraîche to the unwashed frying pan and gently heat. Add
half the cheese and stir until melted.

Measure the cornflour into a bowl, add 4 tablespoons of water and add a
little of the hot crème fraîche and stir. Pour into the frying pan and heat
until the sauce has thickened.

Stir in the lemon juice and season with salt and pepper (the sauce will be
quite thick at this stage). Pour the sauce over the eggs and sprinkle with
breadcrumbs and the remaining cheese.

Bake in the preheated oven for 25–30 minutes until lightly golden and the
salmon is cooked through.

Serve with crusty bread and a dressed salad.

Seafood paella

SERVES 6

1 tbsp oil

1 large onion, roughly chopped

100g (4 oz) chorizo, finely diced

2 cloves garlic, crushed

a pinch of saffron

250g (9 oz) paella rice or easy
cook rice

75ml (2½ fl oz) white wine

600ml (1 pint) fish stock

2 medium tomatoes, roughly
chopped

6 large shell-on raw prawns

6 scallops, quartered

200g (7 oz) squid, sliced into large
pieces

6 large cooked mussels

juice of ½ lemon

1 tbsp chopped fresh parsley

To prepare ahead
Not suitable for cooking ahead
or freezing.

To cook in the Aga
Cook on the boiling plate,
cover and transfer to the
simmering oven for about
20–25 minutes. Continue on
the boiling plate.

*A lovely sociable dish as you can serve it from the pan or
pass a large dish around the table. Add more shellfish if
you are feeling generous. If you don't like squid, replace it
with more prawns.*

Heat the oil in a deep frying pan or paella dish, add the onion and fry
over a high heat for about 5 minutes. Add the chorizo and garlic and fry
until the chorizo is crisp. Add the saffron and rice and toss together for a
few minutes.

Pour over the wine and stock and bring to the boil. Add the tomatoes and
prawns – pushing the prawns down into the liquid. Cover with a lid and
simmer over a low heat for about 15–20 minutes without stirring until
most of the liquid has been absorbed and the rice and prawns are nearly
tender.

Add the scallops, squid and mussels and gently mix. Cover and continue
to simmer for a further 5–10 minutes, or until the seafood and rice are
cooked.

Add the lemon juice and parsley and season with salt and pepper.

Serve hot.

Baked salmon with fennel and tomato

SERVES 6

4 whole fennel bulbs

3 large onions

6 medium tomatoes

4 tbsp olive oil

6 x 150g (5½ oz) middle cut
   salmon fillets, skinned

finely grated zest and juice of 2
   lemons

4 tbsp chopped fresh
   flat-leaf parsley

To prepare ahead
The dish can be prepared and
initial cooking done up to
8 hours ahead – adding the
salmon fillets, lemon juice and
zest before baking as detailed
(right) to serve. Not suitable
for freezing.

To cook in the Aga
Bake the vegetables on the
second set of runners in the
roasting oven for about 12
minutes and a further 12
minutes with the salmon.

---

*A lighter Sunday lunch, which is ideal for a warm sunny day
in the summer – all very healthy.*

Preheat the oven to 200°C/Fan 180°C/Gas 6.

Trim the tops from the fennel bulbs and cut each bulb into 6 wedges.
Cut the onions into similar sized pieces.

Cook the fennel and onions in boiling salted water for about 10 minutes
until just tender and drain well.

Peel the tomatoes and cut into quarters. Remove and discard the seeds.
Mix the tomato wedges with the fennel and onions and pour over the oil.
Toss together and season with salt and pepper. Arrange in the base of an
ovenproof dish and bake in the preheated oven for 15 minutes.

Remove the dish from the oven. Season the salmon fillets and nestle them
among the vegetables. Pour over the lemon juice and sprinkle with the
zest. Bake for a further 15 minutes, or until the fish is just done.

Sprinkle generously with chopped fresh parsley and serve piping hot.

Veggie mains

Broad bean, pea and asparagus risotto

SERVES 6

1.2 litres (2 pints) chicken or
   vegetable stock

2 tbsp olive oil

1 large onion, finely chopped

2 cloves garlic, crushed

350g (12 oz) risotto rice

100g (4 oz) frozen baby broad
   beans

100g (4 oz) frozen petit pois

100g (4 oz) asparagus tips

225g (8 oz) button mushrooms

75g (3 oz) Parmesan cheese,
   coarsely grated, plus extra
   shavings to serve

a small bunch of fresh mint, finely
   chopped

a handful of pea shoots

To prepare ahead
Prepare all the ingredients ahead
and cook and refresh the green
vegetables. Cook and serve at
once. Not suitable for freezing.

To cook in the Aga
Cook the onions, garlic and
rice on the boiling plate. Add
2 tablespoons of hot stock, fry
for a minute and then add the
mushrooms and the remaining
stock. Cover and transfer to
the simmering oven for about
20 minutes. Return to the
simmering plate and stir in the
green vegetables.

*A great summer Sunday lunch when you want to be outside
and just slip indoors for half an hour to cook lunch.*

Measure the stock into a saucepan and bring to the boil.

Heat the oil in a large deep frying pan or saucepan. Add the onion and
garlic and fry over a high heat for about 4 minutes. Add the rice and
coat the grains in the oil and onion mixture.

Lower the heat and spoon two ladles of hot chicken stock into the pan
and stir until most of the stock has been absorbed. Keep adding the
hot stock, stirring, until the rice is nearly cooked – this will take about
12–15 minutes.

Meanwhile, bring a saucepan of salted water to the boil. Add the broad
beans, peas and asparagus and boil for 4 minutes. Drain and refresh in
cold water.

Slice the mushrooms and add to the rice and stir until just cooked.

Add the green vegetables, Parmesan and mint and season with salt and
pepper. The rice should be cooked after 20 minutes (there should be a
little bite to each grain, do not overcook) and the risotto should be light
and creamy.

Serve at once with extra shavings of Parmesan and garnish with pea
shoots.

Fresh tomato, chilli and basil linguine

SERVES 6

2 tbsp oil

1 medium onion, finely chopped

3 cloves garlic, crushed

1 small red chilli, finely chopped

600g (1 lb 5 oz) ripe fresh tomatoes

1 tbsp balsamic vinegar

1 tbsp caster sugar

350g (12 oz) linguine pasta

4 tbsp capers

3 tbsp chopped fresh basil

To prepare ahead
The tomato sauce can be made and whizzed up to 3 days ahead and kept in the fridge. The sauce freezes well, too.

To cook in the Aga
Cook the tomato sauce, covered, in the simmering oven for about 15 minutes.

Use the freshest, reddest, most perfectly ripe tomatoes to give the best colour and flavour. You can use large or baby tomatoes, whichever you have grown or are the finest you can buy. Full of flavour and freshness, this recipe is perfect for a summer Sunday lunch.

Heat the oil in a large frying pan, add onion and gently fry over a high heat for about 5 minutes until tinged golden and soft. Add the garlic and chilli and fry for a further 2 minutes.

Cut the tomatoes into quarters (or 6 if very large). Add to the onion mixture and fry for a minute. Stir in the balsamic vinegar and sugar and season with salt and pepper. Cover, lower the heat and simmer for about 10–15 minutes, or until the tomatoes have broken down and are soft. Whiz until smooth with a hand blender or tip into a processor.

Cook the linguine in boiling salted water according to packet instructions. Drain, add to the hot tomato sauce with 1 tablespoon of the cooking water and the capers. Check the seasoning.

Toss together and serve immediately, sprinkled with basil.

Mushroom and double cheese pasta bake

SERVES 6

1 large onion, roughly chopped

225g (8 oz) penne or shell pasta

2 tbsp olive oil

500g (1 lb 2 oz) mixed
    mushrooms, thickly sliced

2 large cloves garlic, crushed

50g (2 oz) butter

50g (2 oz) flour

300ml (½ pint) milk

300ml (½ pint) double cream

1 tbsp fresh thyme leaves,
    chopped

175g (6 oz) Parmesan cheese

100g (4 oz) Gruyère cheese

To prepare ahead
It can be assembled in the
dish up to 8 hours ahead and
cooked in a preheated oven
200°C/Fan 180°C/Gas 6 for
about 20 minutes to serve.
If making ahead, refresh the
pasta and onion in cold water.
Not suitable for freezing.

To cook in the Aga
Cook on the top set of
runners in the roasting
oven for about 15 minutes
(if serving from hot) or 30
minutes (if made ahead).

A great dish for vegetarians. It's easy to make ahead so you'll just have to pop it in the oven to cook. Then all you'll need is a dressed salad to serve with it. Use a variety of mushrooms, like oyster, shiitake, chestnut and button.

You will need a 1.2 litre (2 pint) ovenproof dish.

Bring a pan of salted water to the boil, add the onion and pasta and boil according to the pasta packet instructions, or until just tender.

While the pasta is cooking, heat the oil in a large frying pan, add the mushrooms and fry over a high heat for about 3 minutes. Add the garlic and fry for a further minute. Drain off any liquid, if necessary.

Melt the butter in a saucepan, add the flour and whisk over a high heat for a minute. Gradually add the milk and cream, whisking until boiled, thick and smooth. Add the thyme leaves, half of each of the cheeses and season with salt and pepper. Stir to combine.

Stir the cooked pasta, onion and mushrooms into the sauce and tip into the ovenproof dish. Level the top and sprinkle over the remaining cheeses.

Slide under the grill for 5–10 minutes until golden and bubbling.

Roasted vegetable and goat's cheese bake

SERVES 4 – 6

2 tbsp olive oil

2 medium red onions, sliced into wedges

2 cloves garlic, crushed

2 medium aubergines, sliced into 2cm (¾ in) cubes

1 yellow pepper, sliced into large dice

2 x 400g can chopped tomatoes

1 tbsp tomato purée

1½ tbsp balsamic vinegar

2 tsp brown sugar

175g (6 oz) hard goat's cheese

100g (4 oz) coarse fresh breadcrumbs

2 tbsp pesto

50g (2 oz) Parmesan cheese, grated

To prepare ahead
Can be assembled up to 8 hours ahead. Cook as detailed (right) to serve. Not suitable for freezing.

To cook in the Aga
Cook the vegetable sauce on the boiling plate for a few minutes, cover and transfer to the simmering oven for about 20 minutes. Roast the completed dish on the second set of runners in the roasting oven for about 30 minutes.

A mixture of aubergine, yellow pepper, tomatoes and goat's cheese with a pesto, cheese and breadcrumb topping. All in one dish, this is ideal for vegetarians.

Preheat the oven to 200°C/Fan 180°C/Gas 6. You will need a 2 litre (3½ pint) shallow ovenproof dish.

Heat the oil in a large frying pan. Add the onions and garlic and fry over a high heat until lightly golden. Add the aubergines and pepper and fry for about 5 minutes until the aubergines are starting to brown and soften.

Stir in the tomatoes, tomato purée, vinegar and sugar, and bring up to the boil. Cover with a lid and simmer for 15 minutes. The vegetables should be soft but still hold their shape. Season with salt and pepper and spoon into the dish.

Cube the goat's cheese and layer on top of the vegetable mixture.

Measure the breadcrumbs and pesto into a bowl and rub together using your hands until the crumbs are coated in the pesto. Sprinkle on top of the goat's cheese and spread out to make an even layer. Sprinkle over the Parmesan cheese.

Bake in the preheated oven for 30 minutes until bubbling around the edges and the crumbs are golden and crispy on top.

Serve with salad and crusty bread.

Pissaladière with onion, herbs and goat's cheese

SERVES 6

200g (7 oz) firm goat's cheese in a roll

1 tbsp olive oil

4 large white onions, roughly chopped

2 cloves garlic

2 red peppers, seeds removed and roughly chopped

1 tsp balsamic vinegar

1 tbsp fresh thyme leaves, chopped

4 large tomatoes, thinly sliced

75g (3 oz) pitted black olives in oil, halved

1 tbsp chopped fresh parsley

Base

175g (6 oz) plain flour

100g (4 oz) butter

25g (1 oz) Parmesan cheese, grated

1 tsp dry mustard

2–3 tbsp water

This is our favourite recipe for lunch at the moment! Serve with a dressed green salad.

Put the goat's cheese into the freezer for about 15 minutes to make it easier to slice.

Measure the oil into a frying pan, add the onions and fry for a couple of minutes over a high heat. Lower the heat, cover and cook for about 10 minutes.

Add the garlic and peppers to the pan, season with salt and pepper, cover again and soften over a low heat for a further 20 minutes until completely soft.

Increase the heat, remove the lid and fry for about 5 minutes until lightly golden. Stir in the vinegar and thyme leaves. Set aside to cool.

Preheat the oven to 220°C/Fan 200°C/Gas 7 and slide in a baking sheet to get hot.

To make the base, measure the flour, butter, Parmesan and mustard into a processor. Season with salt and pepper and whiz until crumbs are formed. Add the water and whiz again until it comes together to form a dough.

Roll out on a floured piece of non-stick baking paper to a diameter of 28cm (11 in) round. Flute the edge and prick the base with a fork.

Spoon the onion mixture on to the base and spread to within 2cm (¾ in) of the edge. Arrange the sliced tomatoes and olives on top.

Remove the hot baking sheet from the oven and slide the paper and tart on to it. Return to the oven and bake for 20–25 minutes until the pastry is lightly golden and the base is crisp.

continued

Remove the goat's cheese from the freezer and cut into 6 slices.

Take the base out of the oven and arrange the goat's cheese on top of the tomatoes. Return to the oven for a further 5–8 minutes, or until the cheese has just melted.

Scatter with the parsley and serve hot.

Spinach and garlic mushroom tartlets

SERVES 8

Pastry

175g (6 oz) plain flour

25g (1 oz) Parmesan cheese, grated

75g (3 oz) butter, cubed

1 large egg

1–2 tbsp water

Filling

a knob of butter

250g (9 oz) small chestnut mushrooms, thickly sliced

2 cloves garlic, crushed

150g (5½ oz) baby spinach

1 large egg

150ml (¼ pint) double cream

50g (2 oz) Parmesan cheese, grated

To prepare ahead
Can be made up to a day ahead and reheated in a moderate oven to heat through. Freezes well cooked.

To cook in the Aga
Cook on the floor of the roasting oven for about 20 minutes or until golden and crisp.

Using small chestnut mushrooms gives a better colour to the tarts. If you don't have a suitable pastry cutter, a saucer will usually do as a guide.

To make the pastry, measure the flour, Parmesan and butter into a processor. Whiz until it looks like breadcrumbs. Add the egg and water and whiz until the pastry just comes together.

Roll out the pastry very thinly on a floured surface. Cut out 8 rounds using an 11cm (4¼ in) round cutter. Line 2 x 4-hole Yorkshire pudding tins with the discs of pastry and leave to chill while you make the filling.

Preheat the oven to 200°C/ Fan 180°C/Gas 6.

Melt the butter in a frying pan. Add the mushrooms and fry over a high heat for 2 minutes. Add the garlic and fry for another 2 minutes. Season and tip out on to a plate. Leave to cool.

Add the spinach to the pan with 1 tablespoon of water. Fry until wilted and season with salt and pepper. Drain any excess liquid, if needed.

Spoon the mushrooms and spinach into the pastry bases.

Crack the egg into a bowl, whisk in the double cream and season with salt and pepper. Pour over the filling in the pastry cases and then sprinkle them all with Parmesan cheese.

Bake in the preheated oven for about 25–30 minutes until lightly golden on top and set in the middle.

Squash and sage gratin

SERVES 6

1kg (2 lb 4 oz) butternut squash, peeled weight

1 large onion, sliced into thin wedges

40g (1½ oz) butter

40g (1½ oz) flour

450ml (16 fl oz) milk

1 tsp Dijon mustard

100g (4 oz) Parmesan cheese

1 tbsp chopped fresh sage leaves

100g (4 oz) breadcrumbs

To prepare ahead
Can be assembled up to 8 hours ahead. Not suitable for freezing.

To cook in the Aga
Slide on to the top set of runners in the roasting oven for about 15 minutes until piping hot.

This is a delicious dish for vegetarians but is also good as a side dish with roast chicken or turkey.

Slice the butternut squash into large 3cm (1¼ in) cubes.

Bring a pan of salted water to the boil, add the squash and onion and boil for about 5 minutes until just tender but still with a bite in the centre. Drain and set aside to keep warm.

Melt the butter in a pan, add the flour and whisk until smooth. Gradually add the milk and continue whisking until thickened and boiling. Add the mustard and half the Parmesan.

Tip the vegetables into a shallow dish and season with salt and pepper. Sprinkle over the sage. Pour over the sauce and scatter with the breadcrumbs. Sprinkle with the remaining cheese.

Slide under a hot grill for about 5 minutes until bubbling and golden.

Serve piping hot.

Vegetable sides

Really good double potato dauphinoise

SERVES 6 – 8

750g (1 lb 10 oz) sweet potatoes, peeled

750g (1 lb 10 oz) King Edward potatoes, peeled

300ml (½ pint) double cream

150ml (¼ pint) chicken or vegetable stock

50g (2 oz) Parmesan cheese, grated

To prepare ahead
Can be part-cooked for about 45 minutes up to 24 hours ahead. To serve, return to the oven (180°C/Fan 160°C/Gas 4) without the foil for about 20–30 minutes, or until piping hot. Freezes well cooked.

To cook in the Aga
Slide on to the second set of runners in the roasting oven for about 30 minutes. Remove the foil and cook for a further 25 minutes.

Dauphinoise potatoes make a nice change with a Sunday lunch, especially if you are serving duck (try them with Duck breasts with cherry sauce *on page 97) or if you are preparing a slighter smarter lunch than usual. To make ahead you need to cook it at once, otherwise the potato slices will turn brown.*

Preheat the oven to 220°C/Fan 200°C/Gas 7. You will need a 2–2.4 litre (3½–4 pint) shallow ovenproof dish, buttered.

Slice the sweet potatoes and King Edwards very thinly using a sharp knife or the slicing blade on a processor.

Arrange one layer of mixed potatoes in the buttered dish. Season with salt and pepper and drizzle over a little double cream and stock.

Continue to layer the potatoes and cream and stock until you have used all the ingredients. Push the potatoes down into the liquid using your hands so they are all covered. Sprinkle with the cheese and cover with foil.

Bake in the preheated oven for about 40 minutes. Remove the foil and continue to cook for another 25–30 minutes, or until golden brown and the potatoes are cooked through.

Leave to stand for 5 minutes before serving.

Roasted Mediterranean vegetables

SERVES 6

2 medium aubergines, sliced into 5cm (2 in) cubes

6 tbsp olive oil

4 medium courgettes, halved and thickly sliced

2 red peppers, deseeded and cut into 2cm (¾ in) cubes

1 medium onion, sliced

2 tbsp balsamic vinegar

3 tbsp fresh basil leaves, chopped

To prepare ahead
Can be made up to 8 hours ahead and served cold or reheated in a large roasting tin in a hot oven for about 15 minutes. Not suitable for freezing.

To cook in the Aga
Roast one tin on the floor of the roasting oven and the other on the second set of runners for 15 minutes. Swap the roasting tin positions and roast for a further 10 minutes.

These are delicious served hot or cold – outside or in. We cook these in two tins to ensure they are chargrilled – if there are too many vegetables piled into one tin they will create too much steam and will be wet and soggy.

Preheat the oven to 220°C/Fan 200°C/Gas 7.

Scatter the aubergine cubes in the base of a roasting tin. Drizzle over 3 tablespoons of the oil and season with salt and pepper.

Put the remaining vegetables in another roasting tin and drizzle with the remaining oil and season with salt and pepper.

Roast both tins in the preheated oven for 30–35 minutes until just soft and tinged brown.

Tip into a serving dish, drizzle with the vinegar, scatter the basil over the top and serve immediately. (To serve cold as a salad, tip into a bowl and leave to cool.)

Parmentier potatoes

SERVES 6

1.5kg (3 lb 5 oz) potatoes, peeled

1 large onion, roughly chopped

100g (4 oz) butter, melted

2 tbsp fresh thyme leaves, chopped

2 cloves garlic, crushed

To prepare ahead
Can be prepared up to 8 hours ahead, ready to roast in the oven as detailed (right). Not suitable for freezing.

To cook in the Aga
Roast on the floor of the roasting oven for 40 minutes. If getting too brown, slide on to the grid shelf on the floor.

These are roasted cubed potatoes with onion, garlic and thyme and make a lovely change from traditional roast potatoes when served with roast meats.

Preheat the oven to 220°C/Fan 200°C/Gas 7 and line a baking sheet with non-stick baking paper.

Cut the potatoes into 2cm (¾ in) cubes. Tip into a pan and cover with salted water. Bring to the boil. Add the onion and boil for 5 minutes. Drain.

Add the butter, thyme and garlic to the empty pan, tip in the drained vegetables and toss lightly until coated. Season with salt and pepper.

Arrange the potatoes and onion in a single layer on the prepared baking sheet. Roast in the preheated oven for 45 minutes until golden and crisp.

New potatoes with salsa verde dressing

SERVES 6 – 8

1kg (2 lb 4 oz) small baby salad
    potatoes, halved

175g (6 oz) sweet pickled
    cucumbers, roughly chopped

Salsa verde dressing

2 spring onions, roughly chopped

3 tbsp roughly chopped fresh
    mint

3 tbsp roughly chopped fresh
    basil leaves

2 tbsp roughly chopped fresh
    parsley leaves

2 tbsp capers

2 anchovy fillets in oil, drained
    and halved

1 clove garlic, crushed

3 tbsp olive oil

3 tbsp mayonnaise

To prepare ahead
Can be made up to 12 hours
ahead. Not suitable for
freezing.

---

*This is a delicious new potato salad that is full of flavour and
improves when it is made ahead. Sweet pickled cucumbers,
sometimes called sweet cucumber spears, come in large 670g
jars and go really well in salads.*

Put the potatoes in a saucepan, cover with salted water and bring to the
boil. Boil for 12–15 minutes, or until just tender. Drain and set aside.

To make the dressing, measure all the ingredients into a bowl and mix
with a hand blender until combined but not too smooth. Check for
seasoning.

Tip the potatoes into a bowl, add the pickled cucumbers and pour over
the dressing. Stir until coated. Cover and leave in the fridge for up to 12
hours to allow the flavours to infuse.

Delicious with cold poached salmon, a barbecued meal or the *Baked
salmon with fennel and tomato* (see page 110).

Caramelised shallots

SERVES 6

2 tbsp oil

450g (1 lb) shallots, peeled

1 dsp light muscovado sugar

1 heaped tsp fresh thyme leaves, chopped

4 tbsp water

2 tbsp balsamic vinegar

To prepare ahead
Can be made up to a day ahead and reheated in a hot oven. Not suitable for freezing.

To cook in the Aga
Start on the boiling plate, transfer to the second set of runners in the roasting oven for about 10 minutes, then transfer to the simmering oven for about 30 minutes until tender. Continue on the boiling plate.

A great side dish to go with any roast. Use pickling onions, if you prefer.

Preheat the oven to 190°C/Fan 170°C/Gas 5.

Heat the oil in a large flameproof casserole, add the shallots and fry over a high heat for about 5 minutes, stirring from time to time.

Add the sugar, thyme and water, and season with salt and pepper. Cover and transfer to the preheated oven for about 25–30 minutes until tender.

Return to the hob, add the vinegar and boil rapidly to reduce the liquid and colour the shallots – they should be golden and sticky.

Serve hot.

Vegetable platter

SERVES 6

2 fennel bulbs

700g (1 lb 9 oz) butternut squash, peeled

500g (1 lb 2 oz) large waxy potatoes, peeled

1 pointed cabbage

25g (1 oz) melted butter

1 clove garlic, crushed

3 tbsp finely chopped fresh parsley

To prepare ahead
The platter can be made up to a day ahead, ready to reheat as detailed (right). Not suitable for freezing.

To cook in the Aga
Slide on to the grid shelf on the floor of the roasting oven for about 20 minutes until piping hot.

These are such a great idea when it's just you in the kitchen and you are entertaining. Everything can be done ahead – including the washing up! Be sure not to overcook when reheating, otherwise the cabbage will lose its colour.

Trim the top and bottom of the fennel bulbs. Slice in half. Cut each half into 3 wedges through the base, keeping the core in so the wedges stay together.

Slice the squash in half and remove the seeds. Cut into 4cm (1½ in) crescent shapes.

Cut the potatoes into 2cm (¾ in) dice.

Slice the cabbage in half, remove the core and roughly shred.

Bring a pan of cold salted water to the boil. Add the fennel, bring back up to the boil and cook for 10 minutes until tender. Remove the fennel from the pan using a slotted spoon (keep the water in the pan) and place in very cold water for 5 minutes. Drain in a colander.

Add the butternut squash to the saucepan of water, bring back up to the boil and cook for 5 minutes. Remove from the pan using a slotted spoon (keep the water in the pan) and place the squash in very cold water for 5 minutes. Drain in a colander.

Repeat the method with the remaining vegetables, cooking the potatoes for about 8 minutes until just tender and the cabbage for 3 minutes.

Brush a large flat platter with a little of the melted butter. Add the garlic and parsley to the remaining butter in the pan and then toss the potatoes in this garlic and parsley butter.

Season all of the vegetables and arrange in piles on the platter. Cover with foil and chill until needed.

To reheat, preheat the oven to 220°C/Fan 200°C/Gas 7 and then roast the platter of vegetables (still covered with foil) for about 25 minutes, checking after 20 minutes that all of the vegetables are hot and steaming.

Slow-cooked red cabbage

SERVES 6

a knob of butter

1 large onion, thinly sliced

1kg (2 lb 4 oz) red cabbage, finely
    shredded

1 cooking apple, peeled, cored
    and thinly sliced

4 tbsp light brown soft sugar

2 tbsp white wine vinegar

2 tbsp redcurrant jelly

To prepare ahead
Can be made and cooked
up to a day ahead and gently
reheated on the hob or in a
dish in a low oven. Freezes well
cooked.

To cook in the Aga
Bring to the boil on the boiling
plate, cover and transfer to the
simmering oven for 2 hours, or
until tender.

So good with red meats and game – try it with Young roast
pheasant *(see page 91) or the* Spiced venison casserole *(see
page 98). Freezes well, too.*

Preheat the oven to 180°C/Fan 160°C/Gas 4.

Melt the butter in a large frying pan. Add the onion and fry over a high
heat for a few minutes.

Wash the cabbage in a colander and add to the pan with the onion.

Tip in the apple, sugar, vinegar and redcurrant jelly and bring to the boil.
Stir and season with salt and pepper. Cover and transfer to the preheated
oven for about 1½–2 hours until the cabbage is tender.

Serve hot or cold.

Carrot and parsnip purée

1kg (2 lb 4 oz) carrots
1kg (2 lb 4 oz) parsnips
a good knob of butter

To prepare ahead
The purée can be made completely the day before and spooned into a dish. Cover and reheat gently in a low oven. Not suitable for freezing.

To cook in the Aga
Bring to the boil on the boiling plate and, after adding the parsnips, boil for a further couple of minutes. Drain, cover with a lid and transfer to the simmering oven for about 20–30 minutes, or until tender.

The purée really does not need garnishing as it is a glorious bright orange colour.

Peel the carrots and cut into small pieces. Tip into a large saucepan, cover with water, add salt and bring to the boil. Boil for 5 minutes.

Peel the parsnips, cut into slightly larger pieces and add to the boiling carrots. Continue to boil for about 15–20 minutes, or until the vegetables are tender.

Drain the vegetables and return them to the saucepan. Heat a little to dry them off. Tip into a processor and whiz until very smooth.

Add the butter, season with salt and pepper and whiz again until smooth.

Tip into a warm serving dish and serve hot.

Celeriac and potato mash

SERVES 6

750g (1 lb 10 oz) King Edward
   potatoes, peeled and cut into
   3cm (1¼ in) cubes
750g (1 lb 10 oz) celeriac, peeled
   and cut into 3cm (1¼ in)
   cubes
1 x 200g tub full-fat crème fraîche

To prepare ahead
The mash can be made up to
6 hours ahead and reheated:
tip it into a buttered, shallow
ovenproof dish, cover with
foil and place in a hot oven
for about 15 minutes, or until
hot through. Not suitable for
freezing.

To cook in the Aga
To reheat, cover with foil and
slide on to the lowest set of
runners in the roasting oven
for about 15 minutes, or until
piping hot.

A wonderful change from the classic mashed potato.

Put the potatoes in a saucepan, cover with cold water, season with salt
and bring to the boil. Boil for about 20 minutes until completely tender.
Drain, return to the pan and mash with a potato masher.

Meanwhile, put the celeriac in a saucepan, cover with cold water, season
with salt and bring to the boil. Boil for about 15 minutes until completely
tender. Drain and tip into a processor. Whiz until smooth and no lumps.

Add the smooth celeriac to the mashed potatoes, season with salt and
pepper, add the crème fraîche and mix well.

Gently warm through in a saucepan and serve immediately.

Roasted parsnip and butternut squash

SERVES 6

25g (1 oz) butter, plus extra for greasing

350g (12 oz) butternut squash, peeled

500g (1 lb 2 oz) parsnips, peeled

25g (1 oz) Parmesan cheese, finely grated

To prepare ahead
Can be made up to 6 hours ahead, ready to pop in the oven as detailed (right). Not suitable for freezing.

To cook in the Aga
Roast on the top set of runners in the roasting oven for 25 minutes.

All in one dish and utterly scrumptious.

Preheat the oven to 220°C/Fan 200°C/Gas 7. Grease an ovenproof dish or a roasting tin with a little butter.

Cut the squash in half lengthways and remove the seeds. Slice the squash into 1½ cm (⅝ in) crescent slices. Slice the parsnips into 1½ cm (⅝ in) pieces.

Boil the vegetables in boiling salted water for 3 minutes. Drain and refresh in cold water.

Add the butter to a large saucepan, melt over a high heat and tip in the vegetables. Season with salt and pepper and lightly toss until coated in the butter.

Spoon into the ovenproof dish and sprinkle with the Parmesan.

Roast in the preheated oven for 25–30 minutes until golden and tender.

Gratin of winter roots and broccoli

SERVES 6

250g (9 oz) parsnips, peeled and
   cut into 3cm (1½ in) cubes

300g (10 oz) butternut squash,
   peeled and cut into 3cm (1½
   in) cubes

250g (9 oz) potatoes, peeled and
   cut into 3cm (1½ in) cubes

2 medium leeks, roughly chopped

1.2 litre (2 pint) vegetable or
   chicken stock

250g (9 oz) broccoli florets

25g (1 oz) butter

25g (1 oz) flour

150ml (¼ pint) milk

2 tbsp full-fat crème fraîche

50g (2 oz) Parmesan cheese,
   coarsely grated

To prepare ahead
Can be made up to 6 hours
ahead and baked as detailed
(right) to serve. Not suitable
for freezing.

To cook in the Aga
Slide the dish on to the second
set of runners in the roasting
oven for 20 minutes.

---

*Delicious to go with any roast and perfect for a
vegetarian, too.*

Preheat the oven to 200°C/Fan 180 °C/Gas 6.

Measure all of the vegetables (except the broccoli) into a large saucepan.
Add the stock and bring to the boil. Boil for about 5 minutes. Add the
broccoli florets and cook for a further 3 minutes.

Pour 150ml (¼ pint) of stock from the pan into a measuring jug and
drain the vegetables. Refresh in cold water and set aside to cool and dry.

Melt the butter in a saucepan over a high heat. Whisk in the flour and
pour in the reserved stock. Whisk until thick. Add the milk and whisk
again. Stir in the crème fraîche and season with salt and pepper.

Arrange the cold, dry vegetables in a shallow ovenproof dish and season
with salt and pepper. Pour over the sauce and sprinkle with the cheese.

Bake in the preheated oven for 20–25 minutes until piping hot and
golden brown on top.

Classic things to go with roasts

Perfect roast potatoes

SERVES 6 - 8

1.5kg (3 lb) King Edward or
   Maris Piper potatoes

100g (4 oz) goose or duck fat

To prepare ahead

Never try to keep roast
potatoes hot in a low oven: it
is better to take them out of
the oven when just perfect
and put them to one side.
Then, just before serving,
re-roast in a very hot oven
for about 10 minutes to crisp,
turning halfway through. You
can use this method and cook
the potatoes up to 8 hours
ahead and reheat to crisp and
serve. They can be frozen but
we are not keen!

To cook in the Aga

Roast on the floor of the
roasting oven for about 45
minutes, according to the size,
turning from time to time.

*The choice of which type potato you use is important as
the floury sort make the fluffier roast potatoes. Goose or
duck fat is best but you could use 100ml (3½ fl oz)
sunflower oil, if preferred.*

Preheat the oven to 200°C/Fan 180°C/Gas 6.

Peel the potatoes and cut each one into even-sized pieces. Transfer to
a large pan and cover with salted water. Bring to the boil quickly with
the lid on, remove the lid and boil rapidly for 5 minutes. Drain well in
a colander. Return the potatoes to the empty pan, replace the lid and
shake the pan to rough up the edges. Season with salt.

Heat the fat in a large roasting tin in the preheated oven for about
3 minutes. Remove the tray from the oven and carefully spoon the
potatoes into the fat and roll them around so they are coated in the hot
fat. Try to space the potatoes out so they are in a single layer and not
touching each other.

Roast in the preheated oven for about 45–50 minutes (for potatoes that
are about 5cm – if they are 8cm, cook for about 1–1¼ hours), turning
every 15 minutes until golden and crisp.

Drain on kitchen paper and serve immediately. Do not cover or they
will go soggy.

Yorkshire pudding

SERVES 8

100g (4 oz) plain flour

¼ tsp salt

3 large eggs

225ml (8 fl oz)
   semi-skimmed milk

approx 125ml (4 fl oz)
   sunflower oil

To prepare ahead
The puddings can be
made completely ahead
and reheated in a hot oven
(temperature as right) for
about 8 minutes. The batter
can be made up to 2 hours
ahead. They freeze well
cooked.

To cook in the Aga
Slide on to the lowest set of
runners in the roasting oven
for about 20 minutes.

---

*My recipe has changed over the years – flours have become
more refined and I find I get the best rise adding more eggs
and omitting a little milk. If you only have full-fat milk,
replace a quarter of the milk with water.*

Preheat the oven to 220°C/Fan 200°C/Gas 7. You will need a 12-hole
deep bun tin or 2 x 4-hole large Yorkshire pudding tins.

Measure the flour and salt into a bowl and make a well in the centre.
Add the eggs and a little milk. Whisk until smooth and gradually add
the remaining milk. This can be made by hand but is best made with an
electric hand whisk until the bubbles burst on the surface. Pour into a
jug.

Measure a dessertspoon of oil into each hole of the 12-hole tin or a
tablespoon in each hole of the 4-hole tins. Transfer to the preheated
oven for about 5 minutes until the oil is piping hot.

Carefully remove from the oven and pour the batter equally between
the holes.

Return to the oven and cook for 20–25 minutes until golden brown
and well risen. Serve immediately.

Sausage and bacon rolls

MAKES 10 ROLLS

5 streaky bacon rashers

10 pork chipolata or cocktail
sausages

To prepare ahead
Can be cooked up to 8 hours
ahead and reheated in a very
hot oven to serve or put back
under the grill to crisp.

To cook in the Aga
To roast the sausage and
bacon rolls, cook on the floor
of the roasting oven for about
20 minutes (for cocktail
sausages) and 30 minutes (for
chipolatas). If you are cooking
the rolls separately, scatter
them around the roast about
30 minutes before the end of
roasting.

*These are very quick and easy, whether you cook the sausage
and bacon separately or make them into a combined sausage
and bacon roll.*

Remove the rind from the bacon rashers and stretch them on a wooden
board using the back of a knife until they are half again of their original
length. Cut each rasher in half horizontally. Wrap each piece around a
cocktail sausage. (If cooking chipolatas, wrap with a whole stretched
piece of bacon.)

Cook at the top of the oven with the roast, if the oven is large enough
– cocktail sausages will take about 20 minutes and chipolatas will take
about 35 minutes.

If you want to cook the sausage and bacon separately, roll up the
stretched rashers of bacon and scatter around the roasting joint
about 30 minutes before the end of roasting or place four on a skewer
and grill for about 4 minutes on each side until golden and crisp.
Meanwhile, grill the sausages or pan fry them until they are golden all
over. You could also scatter them around the roast 15 minutes before
the end of roasting to give added flavour, if liked.

Lemon, thyme and sausagemeat stuffing

SERVES 6

25g (1 oz) butter

1 small onion, finely chopped

450g (1 lb) pork sausagemeat

finely grated rind and juice
   of 1 lemon

2 tbsp chopped fresh parsley

1 tbsp fresh thyme leaves,
   chopped

2 tsp Dijon mustard

To prepare ahead
The stuffing can be made up
to 2 days ahead and kept in
the fridge ready to roast. If
using to stuff a bird, it can be
stuffed with the stuffing the
day before roasting. Freezes
well uncooked.

This is a stuffing I have been making for years and it is still the family's favourite. You can cook this in the two ways shown below or in a buttered ovenproof dish in a hot oven for about 40 minutes.

Add the butter and onion to a frying pan and fry for a couple of minutes over a high heat. Cover, lower the heat and cook for about 15 minutes, or until tender. Tip into a mixing bowl.

Add the remaining ingredients to the bowl, season with salt and pepper and mix well to combine.

Use to stuff the breast end of a turkey or chicken (do not put in the cavity of any bird), or shape into 12 round balls and arrange around the roast to cook at the same time for about 20 minutes.

Sage and onion stuffing

450g (1 lb) onions, coarsely chopped

75g (3 oz) butter, melted, plus a little extra for buttering the dish

225g (8 oz) fresh coarse white breadcrumbs

2 good tbsp chopped fresh sage

2 tbsp chopped fresh parsley

To prepare ahead
Can be made a day ahead and reheated in a hot oven (200°C/Fan 180°C/Gas 6) for about 10–15 minutes. Freezes well uncooked.

To cook in the Aga
Bake the dish on the top set of runners in the roasting oven for about 20 minutes.

A classic stuffing to serve with duck, pork or goose – I like to cook it in a thin layer in a wide dish, which gives a nice crispy top.

Butter an oblong ovenproof dish about 20 x 26cm (8 x 10½ in).

Put the onion pieces into a saucepan, cover with 300ml (½ pint) water and bring to the boil. Boil for 15 minutes until tender. Drain and tip the onions into a mixing bowl.

Add the remaining ingredients to the bowl, season with salt and pepper and mix until combined. Spoon into the buttered dish and spread evenly to give a thin layer, but don't press down – leave fluffy.

Bake in the oven alongside your roast for 20–25 minutes until pale golden brown and crispy on top.

Serve hot with your roast.

Gravy to go with roasts

SERVES 6

1 small onion or shallot, finely
   chopped

1 tbsp plain flour

425ml (¾ pint) hot stock or
   vegetable water

To prepare ahead

If you anticipate feeling a bit
pushed for time just before
serving, you can prepare the
base of the gravy in advance
up to a day ahead. For 4
people, heat 1 tablespoon of
oil in a pan, add ½ chopped
onion and fry for a few
minutes. Blend in 25g (1 oz)
flour and stir for a minute.
Pour in 300ml (½ pint) stock
and bring to the boil, stirring
all the time. Strain and keep
chilled until needed. This base
can then be poured into the
roasting tin while the meat is
resting to make a quick gravy.

---

*Gravy is an essential accompaniment for all roast meats,
game and poultry. Stock is required for all gravies and if
home-made stock is not available, a stock cube and boiling
water or vegetable cooking water may be used. If your gravy
looks a little pale there is no shame to adding a little gravy
browning (natural caramel). Beef and lamb gravies are
greatly enriched by adding red wine as part of the liquid
quantity. Rarely is there any red wine left to add to gravy in
our house, though! The answer for me is to take a bottle of
red wine and reduce it by two thirds by boiling it in a shallow
large pan. Cool it and then keep it in the fridge for up to two
months ready to use to perk up gravies, casseroles and sauces.
You need to use less reduced wine than the amount of wine
specified in a recipe since it has a more intense flavour.*

Remove the joint from the oven and transfer to a warmed plate to rest
before carving.

Skim the surplus fat from the roasting tin, leaving about 1 tablespoon
in the tin. Add the onion or shallot and fry on the hob for a couple of
minutes.

Sprinkle in the flour and stir well, scraping up any sediment and juices
in the bottom of the tin.

Stir in the stock or vegetable water (hot will make it boil quicker). Bring
to the boil, stirring well, and boil for 2–3 minutes. Strain into a gravy
boat and serve.

Beef gravy

Add a good teaspoon of tomato purée and a tablespoon of Worcestershire sauce as the gravy comes to the boil after adding the stock.

Lamb gravy

Add a tablespoon of Worcestershire sauce, a tablespoon of redcurrant jelly and a sprig of rosemary as the gravy comes to the boil after adding the stock.

Pork gravy

Add a tablespoon of apple sauce as the gravy comes to the boil after adding the stock. If you have apple juice to hand, though, you could replace some of the stock with this. Make the gravy a little thicker, if you prefer, by increasing the fat and flour to 1½ tablespoons.

Game gravy

This gravy should be fairly thin and well flavoured, therefore flour is not always used. The best game gravy is made using the stock from the game you are cooking. Add a little Worcestershire sauce and redcurrant jelly, too, or Port or red wine, if liked.

Bread sauce

SERVES 6

1 medium onion, peeled and cut
    into quarters

6 black peppercorns

1 bay leaf

600ml (1 pint) full-fat milk

100g (4 oz) fresh fine white
    breadcrumbs

a knob of butter

a fine grating of nutmeg

To prepare ahead

The sauce can be made up to
2 hours ahead and covered
with cling film to prevent a
skin forming. If after it stands
it is a little thick, add a touch
more milk. It freezes well –
once thawed, reheat on the
hob, adding a little more milk
until the right consistency is
reached.

To cook in the Aga

Bring the sauce and
flavourings to boiling point,
cover and transfer to the
simmering oven for about 20
minutes to infuse, or sit on the
back of the Aga for about 30
minutes.

---

*A perfect accompaniment to chicken and turkey. Avoid
keeping bread sauce hot for a long time as it turns grey in
colour.*

Place the onion, peppercorns and bay leaf in a saucepan. Pour in the
milk and gently heat until it reaches boiling point. Remove from the
heat, cover with a lid and set aside for the flavours to infuse for about 30
minutes.

Using a slotted spoon remove the onion and bay leaf and scoop out the
peppercorns. Stir the breadcrumbs into the milk, add the butter and
nutmeg and season with salt and a little pepper. Stir until combined.

Serve warm.

White onion sauce

SERVES 6

25g (1 oz) butter

1 medium onion, finely chopped

25g (1 oz) flour

300ml (½ pint) hot milk

> **To prepare ahead**
> Can be made up to 4 hours
> ahead and kept warm or
> reheated on the hob – you
> may need to add a touch more
> milk if reheating. Not suitable
> for freezing.

Onion sauce is delicious in winter with lamb or mutton when there is no fresh mint about.

Melt the butter in a small saucepan over a high heat. Add the onion and cook for a minute. Lower the heat, cover with a lid and cook for about 20 minutes, or until the onion is soft but not coloured.

Sprinkle in the flour and stir until combined.

Blend in the hot milk, stirring continuously, and bring to the boil until thickened and smooth. Season with salt and pepper.

Serve hot on its own or over leeks.

Fresh horseradish sauce

SERVES 6

150ml (¼ pint) double cream

2 level tbsp grated horseradish

1 tsp white wine vinegar

a little caster sugar to taste

> **To prepare ahead**
> The sauce can be made
> completely up to 3 days
> ahead. Check seasoning and
> sharpness before serving.
> It can be frozen but, once
> thawed, add a little more
> whipped cream to make it
> smooth again.

Freshly grated home-grown horseradish would be best, but long-life grated horseradish can be bought in glass jars from the supermarket. All you need to do is add cream, vinegar and sugar for a really good home-made sauce to serve with beef.

Light whip the cream and stir in the horseradish.

Add the vinegar, a little sugar to taste and season with salt and pepper. Stir until thoroughly mixed.

Turn into a serving bowl, cover with cling film and chill before serving.

Fresh cranberry sauce

SERVES 8

225g (8 oz) fresh cranberries

300g (10 oz) caster sugar

finely grated rind and juice of 1
    large orange

To prepare ahead
Can be made up to a day
ahead and kept in the fridge.
Not suitable for freezing.

*A lovely fresh-tasting sauce as the cranberries are raw. It has
a bright scarlet colour, too. It is a classic with turkey but is
also delicious with a variety of cold meats, especially game.*

Place all the ingredients in the processor and whiz until smooth. Serve
cold or heat gently to serve warm.

Fresh mint sauce

SERVES 6

a large bunch of fresh mint

1–2 tbsp caster sugar

2–3 tbsp boiling water

1–2 tbsp white wine vinegar

To prepare ahead
Can be made up to 2 days
ahead – keep it in a jar in
the fridge. Not suitable for
freezing.

*A traditional accompaniment to roast lamb, lamb cutlets and
chops, it is much tastier freshly made than bought from a jar.
I prefer apple mint but you can use whatever mint variety you
have growing in your garden.*

Strip the mint leaves from the stalks and finely chop the leaves.

Tip into a pan, add the sugar and pour in the boiling water. Stir for
about 2–3 minutes.

Add the vinegar to taste and set aside to stand for about an hour to
allow the flavours to infuse before serving.

Bramley apple sauce

SERVES 6–10

450g (1 lb) Bramley apples

3 tbsp water

juice of ½ lemon

25g (1 oz) granulated sugar

a knob of butter

To prepare ahead
Can be made up to a day
ahead. Freezes well.

To cook in the Aga
Start on the boiling plate,
cover and transfer to the
simmering oven for about 30
minutes.

I used to make apple sauce by just roughly chopping the apples, skins and all, then stewing and sieving them, thinking that by adding the skins it would give a lovely green colour to the sauce. Not so and you have a messy sieve to wash up! Now, more often than not, I use windfalls and peel and core them first.

Peel and core the apples, removing any bruised bits. Roughly chop the flesh and tip into a pan with the water and lemon juice.

Cover with a tight fitting lid and gently cook over a low heat for about 20 minutes, stirring from time to time until the apples are very soft.

Take off the heat and beat well with a wooden spoon until smooth.

Add the sugar and taste – if you like it a bit sweeter, add a touch more.

Stir in the knob of butter – the apples should still be warm enough to melt the butter.

Spoon into a bowl and serve cold with roast pork, goose, pheasant or duck.

Hollandaise sauce

SERVES 6

6 tbsp white wine vinegar

1 bay leaf

a few parsley stalks

6 peppercorns

225g (8 oz) unsalted butter

4 large egg yolks

To prepare ahead
Can be made up to 2 days ahead and reheated very gently on the hob to serve warm (be careful not to overheat otherwise it may split). Not suitable for freezing.

Make this to serve with salmon, asparagus and fish dishes: try it with the Stuffed fillets of sole on a bed of spinach *(see page 104). If you have a large processor or are making a small quantity, it is a good idea to warm the bowl first by filling it with boiling water, as you would heat a teapot. If you have to use salted butter, when you melt the butter do not use the milky solids at the bottom of the saucepan.*

Measure the vinegar into a pan and add the bay leaf, parsley stalks and peppercorns. Bring to the boil and reduce to about 1 tablespoon. Strain through a sieve into a jug.

Melt the butter in the saucepan.

Warm the bowl of the processor with boiling water and then throw the water away. Put in the egg yolks, pour over the hot vinegar and whiz until smooth. With the machine still running add the hot butter by pouring it through the funnel slowly.

When all the butter has been added, season with salt and pepper. Taste – it should be lightly piquant (if it is not sharp enough add a squeeze of lemon juice).

Serve cold or lukewarm.

Béarnaise sauce

SERVES 6

8 tbsp white wine vinegar

2 shallots, peeled and cut in half

1 bay leaf

a few parsley stalks, plus 1 tbsp
    chopped fresh parsley

6 peppercorns

225g (8 oz) unsalted butter

4 large egg yolks

1 tbsp chopped fresh tarragon

To prepare ahead
Can be made up to 2 days
ahead and reheated very
gently on the hob to serve
warm (be careful not to
overheat otherwise it may
split). Not suitable for
freezing.

*First cousin to Hollandaise, Béarnaise sauce has added
fresh herbs and is delicious with hot fillet of beef, steaks
and shellfish.*

Measure the vinegar into a pan and add the shallots, bay leaf, parsley
stalks and peppercorns. Bring to the boil and reduce to about 2
tablespoons. Strain through a sieve into a jug.

Melt the butter in the saucepan.

Warm the bowl of the processor with boiling water and then throw the
water away. Put in the egg yolks, pour over the hot vinegar and whiz
until smooth. With the machine still running add the hot butter by
pouring it through the funnel slowly.

When all the butter has been added, season with salt and pepper and
stir in the chopped fresh parsley and tarragon.

Serve cold or lukewarm.

Garlic cream sauce

SERVES 4–6

3 bulbs garlic, peeled

250ml (9 fl oz) full-fat crème
fraîche

2 anchovies in oil, drained and
chopped

2 tbsp hot stock

> **To prepare ahead**
> Can be made up to a day
> ahead – note the flavours
> will infuse and be stronger if
> made ahead. Can be served
> hot or cold – if you prefer it
> hot, gently reheat in a pan
> on the hob. Not suitable for
> freezing.

Perfect with slow-roast shoulder of lamb (see Lamb
boulangère *on page 60) or roast chicken.*

Slice the garlic bulbs in half horizontally and sit in the roasting tin
under the lamb or chicken.

Once the meat is cooked, transfer to a plate to rest. Sit the roasting tin
on the hob and skim off any fat. Add the crème fraîche, anchovies and
stock and bring to the boil, whisking the sediment and squashed soft
garlic into the sauce.

Season with salt and pepper, strain through a sieve into a jug and serve.

Dill and mustard cream sauce

SERVES 4 – 6

4 tbsp white wine vinegar

1 shallot, finely chopped

1 bay leaf

4 black peppercorns

1 sprig of fresh thyme

2–3 tbsp Dijon mustard

1 x 200ml tub full-fat crème fraîche

4 tbsp snipped fresh chives

2–3 tsp caster sugar

To prepare ahead
Can be made up to 2 days ahead and kept chilled. Not suitable for freezing.

Perfect with cold fillet of beef, sirloin or cold ham. You can add more or less mustard to taste.

Measure the vinegar into a saucepan and add the shallot, bay leaf, peppercorns and thyme. Bring to the boil until the vinegar has reduced by half. Strain the liquid through a sieve and set aside to become cold. Discard the flavourings.

Blend the mustard, crème fraîche, chives, sugar and vinegar reduction together in a bowl and season with salt and pepper.

Serve chilled.

Cumberland sauce

SERVES 6 – 8

2 shallots, finely chopped

finely shredded rind and juice of 1 large orange

finely shredded rind of 1 large lemon

225g (8 oz) redcurrant jelly

75ml (2½ fl oz) Port

1 tsp Dijon mustard

1 heaped tsp cornflour

1 tbsp red or white wine vinegar

> **To prepare ahead**
> The sauce can be completely made up to a week ahead and gently reheated on the hob to serve. Not suitable for freezing.

Delicious with cold ham, bacon joints, cold lamb and game: try it with Gammon with a ginger glaze *on page 180.*

Put the shallots into a saucepan and add the orange rind and juice and the lemon rind. Pour in 75ml (2½ fl oz) water. Bring to the boil and simmer for about 5 minutes. Drain and reserve the shallot and rinds, discarding the cooking liquid.

Spoon the redcurrant jelly into a saucepan, add the Port and gently heat until the jelly is melted.

Measure the mustard, cornflour and vinegar into a bowl and mix together (if it is a little thick, add some water to give a smooth paste). Add to the saucepan with the jelly and stir until slightly thickened.

Add the reserved shallot and rinds and season to taste.

Serve hot or cold.

Winter curry

Malay lamb curry

SERVES 4 – 6

2 tbsp oil

900g (2 lb) diced leg of lamb

2 large onions, sliced

3 tbsp red Thai paste

½ red chilli, deseeded and cut
    into four

6cm (2½ in) piece root ginger,
    peeled and cut into small cubes

finely grated rind and juice of 1
    lime

1 tsp ground cinnamon

2 tbsp flour

1 x 400ml can coconut milk

100ml (3½ fl oz) water

2 tsp fish sauce

1 tbsp brown sugar

3 star anise

1 small stick lemon grass, bashed

4 dried lime leaves

To prepare ahead
Can be made up to 2 days
ahead and reheated on the
hob or in a low oven. Freezes
well cooked. If too thick when
thawed, add a little more water.

To cook in the Aga
Bring to the boil, cover and
transfer to the simmering oven
for about 2 hours, or until
tender.

*The ingredients list may seem long but curries have a large
number of ingredients by tradition. It is well worth making
the effort to find them since they all play an important part
in giving the final dish its wonderful flavour.*

Preheat the oven to 180°C/Fan 160°C/Gas 4.

Place 1 tablespoon of the oil in a large flameproof casserole over a high
heat. Add the diced lamb and brown all over (you may need to do this
in batches). Remove using a slotted spoon and transfer to a plate.

Add the remaining oil to the pan, stir in the onions and fry for about 4
minutes until starting to soften.

Meanwhile, measure the Thai paste, chilli, ginger and lime rind and
juice into a small processor or blender and whiz until finely chopped.

Add the curry paste mixture to the pan and fry for 3–4 minutes.

Sprinkle in the cinnamon and flour and blend in the coconut milk
and water, stirring all the time. Bring to the boil and add the fish sauce,
sugar, star anise, lemon grass and lime leaves. Season with salt and
pepper.

Return the lamb to the pan, bring back to the boil, cover and transfer to
the preheated oven for about 1½ hours, or until the lamb is tender.

Remove the star anise, lemon grass and lime leaves, check the seasoning
and serve with *Jasmine rice* (see page 166).

Fragrant chicken curry

SERVES 6

2 tbsp oil

12 chicken thighs, skinned, boned
and cut into 4 pieces

2 large onions, roughly chopped

2 tbsp garam masala

1 tbsp ground coriander

1 x 400g can chopped tomatoes

1 x 400g can coconut milk

2 tbsp tamarind paste

1 stick fresh lemon grass, bashed

Curry paste

6cm (2½ in) fresh root ginger,
peeled and cut into small
cubes

2 shallots, peeled and quartered

1–2 red chillies, deseeded and
roughly chopped

4 cloves garlic, peeled

To prepare ahead
Can be made up to a day
ahead and reheated on the
hob to serve. Freezes well
cooked.

To cook in the Aga
Bring to the boil on the
boiling plate, cover and
transfer to the simmering
oven for about an hour.

---

*This curry is fragrant and not hot, just a wonderful
combination of flavours. If it is heat that you like, though, add
more chilli and garam masala. It can be cooked in the oven at
160°C/Fan 140°C/Gas 3 for 45 minutes, if you prefer.*

First make the paste – measure all the ingredients into a small processor
or blender and whiz until finely chopped.

Place the oil in a large deep frying pan over a high heat. Add the
chicken pieces and brown until golden on all sides. Remove with a
slotted spoon and set aside.

Add the onions to the pan and fry for about 4 minutes until starting to
soften.

Stir in the curry paste and spices and fry for a further 2 minutes.
Return the chicken to the pan and stir to cover in the paste mixture.

Tip in the remaining ingredients, season with salt and pepper and
bring to the boil, stirring. Cover and cook gently on the hob for about
45 minutes, or until the chicken is tender and the sauce is a rich, light
brown colour.

Remove from the heat and discard the lemon grass. Serve hot with rice
(see page 166).

Prawn korma-style curry

SERVES 6

2 tbsp sunflower oil

1 large onion, roughly chopped

4cm (1½ in) fresh ginger, peeled
and finely grated

1 red pepper, deseeded and cut
into small dice

1 tsp cardamom seeds, crushed

1½ tbsp ground cumin

1½ tbsp ground coriander

1½ tbsp garam masala

1 x 400ml can coconut milk

150ml (¼ pint) chicken stock

2 tsp caster sugar

juice of 1 lemon

100g (4 oz) ground almonds

800g (1 lb 12 oz) shelled raw tiger
prawns

To prepare ahead
The sauce can be made a day
ahead, adding the almonds
and prawns when you reheat
on the hob. Not suitable for
freezing.

*This has a wonderful, intense flavour. The raw prawns are
added at the last minute to stop them overcooking. Make sure
not to cover the pan with a lid, otherwise the sauce
will not reduce.*

Heat the oil in a deep frying pan. Add the onion and fry gently for
about 20 minutes until tender.

Add the ginger and pepper and fry for a minute or so.

Sprinkle in the cardamom seeds and spices and fry for another minute.

Stir in the coconut milk, stock, sugar and lemon juice. Season with salt
and pepper, and simmer over a low heat for about 5 minutes until the
sauce has reduced slightly.

Stir in the almonds and prawns and cook over a high heat for about
3 minutes, or until the prawns have turned pink and are cooked
through.

Serve at once with rice (see page 166).

Just-boiled rice

SERVES 4 – 6

225g (8 oz) long grain easy
    cook rice

350ml (12 fl oz) water

1 tsp salt

To prepare ahead
Can be made on the day
and reheated in a dish in a
moderate oven. Not suitable
for freezing.

To cook in the Aga
Bring to the boil on the boiling
plate. Cover and transfer to the
simmering oven for about 20
minutes until the liquid has
been absorbed and the rice is
tender.

*For something a bit different, you could transform this recipe
into a very delicious Spiced Coriander Rice by following the
instructions below but adding ¼ teaspoon each of ground
cumin, ground coriander and turmeric at the beginning.
Once cooked, stir in 2 tablespoons of chopped fresh coriander
leaves and serve.*

Measure the ingredients into a saucepan, bring to the boil, cover with a
lid and simmer over a gentle heat for about 15 minutes until tender and
the liquid has been absorbed.

Serve hot or cold.

Jasmine rice

SERVES 4 – 6

225g (8 oz) jasmine rice

1 x 400ml can coconut milk

150ml (¼ pint) water

½ tsp finely grated fresh ginger

1 stick lemon grass, bashed

*This is very sticky rice but it is a classic and makes a delicious
accompaniment to any curry.*

Measure all the ingredients into a saucepan. Season with salt and bring
to the boil. Cover with a lid and simmer very gently over a low heat for
about 15–20 minutes, or until all the liquid has been absorbed.

Remove the lemon grass and discard. Serve hot.

Aromatic green beans

SERVES 4–6

500g (1 lb 2 oz) French green
   beans, topped and tailed

6 tbsp pouring double cream

½ tsp ground coriander

½ tsp ground cumin

2 cloves garlic, crushed

To prepare ahead
Beans can be cooked up to
8 hours ahead and kept in
the fridge. Toss in the cream
and serve immediately. Not
suitable for freezing.

A colourful and lightly spiced accompaniment to curry.

Cut each bean into four. Bring a pan of salted water to the boil, add the beans and boil for 4 minutes. Drain and refresh in cold water.

Heat the cream in the saucepan, add the spices and garlic and then toss in the beans to heat them through. Season with salt and pepper.

Serve at once so that the beans keep their colour.

Side dishes for curry

These dishes (also called sambals*) are great accompaniments for any curry party. A few other ideas include: a bowl of plain desiccated coconut, which goes well with spicy curry; coarsely chopped or sliced hard-boiled eggs; a variety of nuts, e.g. peanuts, cashew nuts, chopped and ground almonds; slices of banana, tossed in lemon juice; and poppadoms and naan bread. All are very good choices and are available from specialist shops or your local supermarkets. Serve them in little dishes with a teaspoon for each and pass them around the table. If you are making very hot curries, be sure to serve the Raita as this is a cooling dish!*

Mango and tomato relish

SERVES 4 – 6

1 large ripe mango

1 tbsp mango chutney

1 large tomato

Finely dice the mango and mix it with the mango chutney to combine.

Remove the seeds from a tomato and finely dice the flesh. Stir into the mango, season with salt and pepper and serve in a bowl.

Lime and coriander relish

SERVES 4 – 6

2 shallots, grated

finely grated zest and juice of 1 small lime

2 tbsp chopped fresh coriander

1 tsp finely chopped fresh green chilli

1 tsp runny honey

Mix all the ingredients together, season with salt and pepper and serve in a bowl.

Raita

1 x 200g tub plain Greek yoghurt

1 heaped tbsp chopped fresh mint

10cm (4 in) cucumber, coarsely
   grated and squeezed to extract
   the juice

Mix together and season with salt and pepper.

Variations

Add a choice from below to the Greek yoghurt and mint:

Onion Raita

Coarsely grated onion, squeezed to extract the juice

Chilli Raita

1 teaspoon of finely chopped green chilli, plus a pinch of chilli powder

Cumin Raita

½ teaspoon of crushed cumin seeds, plus 2 teaspoons of fresh
coriander

Ginger Raita

2 teaspoons of chopped pickled ginger, plus 1 teaspoon grated fresh
root ginger

Mango Raita

1 tablespoon of mango chutney, 1 tablespoon of lemon juice and a
little chopped ripe mango

Summer buffet

Chicken, pear, Parmesan and rocket salad

SERVES 6

1 x 80g packet rocket

2 small courgettes

75g (3 oz) Parmesan cheese

2 large chicken breasts, cooked

2 ripe pears, peeled

juice of ½ lemon

Dressing

2 tbsp balsamic vinegar

4 tbsp olive oil

1 tbsp Dijon mustard

1 tsp caster sugar

> **To prepare ahead**
> The salad can be assembled
> up to 6 hours ahead. Add
> the pears and dressing just
> before serving. Not suitable
> for freezing.

An unusual combination of ingredients, perhaps, but this is a delicious salad that would be good as part of a summer buffet.

Scatter the rocket over a large flat serving plate. Using a potato peeler, peel ribbons of courgette and Parmesan over the top.

Slice the chicken breasts and place them on the salad.

Cut the pears in half, remove the core and thinly slice. Toss the pear slices in the lemon juice and scatter over the salad.

Measure all the dressing ingredients into a bowl and whisk together. Pour over the salad, toss and serve.

Tomato and mango chilled chicken

SERVES 4 – 6

500g (1 lb 2 oz) chicken breast,
    cooked and sliced into thin
    strips
1 tbsp snipped fresh chives

Sauce

2 tbsp tomato chutney

2 tbsp smooth mango chutney

4 spring onions, finely sliced

4 heaped tbsp light mayonnaise

4 heaped tbsp half fat or full fat
    crème fraiche

a dash of lemon juice

To prepare ahead
Can be made up to a day
ahead. Not suitable for
freezing.

*Dead easy to make and great with a green salad and crusty
bread for a summer's day.*

Measure all the sauce ingredients into a bowl and season with salt and
pepper. Mix to combine.

Add the chicken to the bowl, coat in the sauce and leave to marinate for
up to 2 hours.

Serve garnished with snipped chives.

Pesto and crème fraîche chicken salad

SERVES 6

750g (1 lb 10 oz) chicken, cooked and shredded into thin strips

some lettuce leaves

Pesto and crème fraîche sauce

1 x 200ml tub crème fraîche

1 x 145g tub fresh basil pesto

1 x 200g tub Greek yoghurt

1 tsp caster sugar

1 tsp lemon juice

100g (4 oz) sweet pickled cucumber spears, sliced, plus a few extra to garnish

To prepare ahead
Chicken can be marinated in the dressing up to a day ahead – assemble with the lettuce before serving. Not suitable for freezing.

We love this easy chicken dish and it is perfect for using up leftover roast chicken from your Sunday roast. It improves with infusing so is better made the day before. Sweet cucumber spears are long wedges of pickled cucumber. Very good with cold meats and salads, they come in large 670g jars.

Measure all the sauce ingredients into a bowl and mix to combine. Season with salt and pepper.

Stir in the chicken and leave to marinate, ideally for 2 hours.

Arrange the lettuce leaves on a platter and spoon the chicken mixture into the centre of the dish. Garnish with the remaining pickles.

Chilled garlic chicken breasts with tomato salad

SERVES 6

a good knob of butter, plus a little extra melted butter for glazing

1 medium onion, finely chopped

2 fat cloves garlic, crushed

100g (4 oz) spinach, coarsely chopped

200g (7 oz) full-fat cream cheese

1 egg yolk

a little grated nutmeg

6 chicken breasts, boneless, skin on

6 large tomatoes, sliced

1 tbsp snipped fresh chives

To prepare ahead
The chicken breasts can be cooked up to a day ahead. Arrange on the platter up to 6 hours ahead. The stuffed raw chicken breasts freeze well for up to 3 months.

To cook in the Aga
Cook the onion in the simmering oven for 20 minutes. Roast the chicken on the second set of runners for about 25 minutes.

These look good sliced on a large flat dish arranged with the tomato salad for a buffet. The chicken is really moist and tasty and can be served hot, if preferred.

Preheat the oven to 200°C/Fan 180°C/Gas 6.

Melt the butter in a frying pan and add the onion. Fry over a high heat for a few minutes. Lower the heat, cover and cook the onion for about 15 minutes, or until soft.

Add the garlic and spinach and stir over a high heat for about 3 minutes until the spinach has just wilted. Check all the moisture has evaporated and then spoon the spinach into a bowl and set aside for about 10 minutes to cool.

Spoon the cream cheese, egg yolk and nutmeg into the bowl of spinach and season with salt and pepper. Stir well to combine and set aside to become stone cold.

Lay the chicken breasts on a board and loosen the skin from one side. Divide the spinach stuffing into six and spoon under the skin in an even layer. Carefully pull the skin back over to cover the stuffing.

Arrange the breasts in a roasting tin in a single layer and brush with a little melted butter. Roast in the preheated oven for about 30 minutes (less if the breasts are small). Set aside to cool.

Arrange the sliced tomatoes on a platter, season with salt and pepper and dress with a pesto dressing (see page 184). Slice each chicken breast into four diagonal slices and arrange in a circle or in lines over the tomatoes. Sprinkle with the chives and serve.

Whole fillet of beef with horseradish and herb sauce

SERVES 6 – 8

1.8 kg (4 lb) whole centre cut fillet
    of beef from the thick end

2 tbsp oil

a good knob of butter

Horseradish and herb sauce

1 x 200ml tub crème fraîche

2 tbsp strong horseradish sauce

2 tbsp light mayonnaise

2 tsp Dijon mustard

2 tbsp chopped fresh dill

3 tbsp chopped fresh parsley

2 tbsp lemon juice

To prepare ahead
To serve hot, brown up to
a day ahead and roast as
detailed (right) to serve. Not
suitable for freezing. The
horseradish and herb sauce
can be made up to 3 days
ahead.

To cook in the Aga
Roast on the second set of
runners in the roasting oven
for 25 minutes.

Perfect hot or cold for a very special occasion. To serve cold, roast up to two days ahead and leave to cool. It can be carved up to five hours ahead. Reassemble the slices and then wrap them in clingfilm until it is time to serve – that way the meat will still be beautifully pink. If you don't, the surface of the meat will turn grey half an hour or so after being exposed to the air.

Preheat the oven to 220°C/Fan 200°C/Gas 7.

Season the beef with salt and pepper and rub the oil over the meat.

Place a frying pan over a high heat until very hot and then brown the beef quickly on all sides. Transfer the fillet to a small roasting tin, spread with a little butter and roast in the preheated oven for about 30 minutes for medium rare (8 minutes per 450g/1 lb). Remove from the oven to rest for about 10 minutes.

To make the sauce, mix all the ingredients together in a bowl and season with salt and pepper.

Carve the meat into thin slices and serve the hot fillet with the cold sauce.

Cold poached salmon with avocado and pickled ginger

SERVES 6

a little melted butter

6 x 150g (5½ oz) middle cut
  salmon fillets, skin on

6 slices smoked salmon

12 slices pickled ginger

1 tablespoon toasted sesame
  seeds

Avocado topping

2 medium ripe avocadoes,
  roughly chopped

1 tsp wasabi paste

juice of ½ lemon

4 tbsp full-fat crème fraîche

To prepare ahead
The salmon fillets can be
cooked up to a day ahead.
The toppings can be arranged
up to 6 hours ahead and kept
covered in the fridge. Not
suitable for freezing.

To cook in the Aga
Cook the salmon in the foil
tent in the simmering oven of
the Aga for about 45 minutes
until cooked through.

---

*An unusual but truly delicious cold summer lunch. Wasabi is
a Japanese paste, similar to horseradish but with an oriental
kick. Pickled ginger comes in a jar of fine pink slices of ginger
– do not confuse it with crystallised ginger! We prefer this
long, slow method of cooking the salmon to fast roasting; it
keeps the salmon moist and succulent.*

Preheat the oven to 140°C/Fan 120°C/Gas 2 and arrange a piece of
foil over a baking tray, double the length but positioned in the middle.
Brush it with melted butter and season with salt and pepper.

Place the salmon fillets, skin side up on the foil. Fold the foil over
and seal around the edges so the salmon are enclosed. Slide into the
preheated oven and bake for about 45 minutes until the salmon is just
cooked through and is a matt pink with no liquid oozing out – keep
checking. Set aside to cool and peel off the skin.

Tip the avocadoes into a processor, add the wasabi, lemon juice and
crème fraîche, season with salt and pepper and whiz until smooth.

Divide the mixture into six and spread over the cold salmon fillets in a
neat even layer. Swirl one piece of smoked salmon in the centre of each
fillet and place a slice of ginger on either side. Sprinkle a few sesame
seeds over the smoked salmon and serve with baby new potatoes and
mangetout or a green salad.

Gammon with a ginger glaze

1.8kg (4 lb) smoked gammon

1.5 litre (2¾ pint) ginger beer

4 bulbs of stem ginger in syrup, finely chopped

2 tsp ground ginger

To prepare ahead

The gammon can be cooked and glazed up to 3 days ahead to serve cold. To serve hot, the gammon can be cooked and skinned 3 days ahead and then glazed and reheated in a hot oven to serve.

To cook in the Aga

Bring the pan to the boil and simmer for 5 minutes, cover and transfer to the simmering oven for about 90 minutes until tender. Spread the glaze over the ham and slide on to the lowest set of runners in the roasting oven for about 20 minutes, or until golden.

The ultimate buffet dish – slice some ahead but also have the whole joint on a board so your guests can see you have made it! We prefer to cook a smaller joint in the oven rather than boiling it on top as we think it shrinks less. If you do not have a pan which will fit in the oven you can simmer it, covered, on the hob for the same timings.

Preheat the oven to 160°C/Fan 140°C/Gas 3.

Place the gammon snugly in a pan. Completely cover with ginger beer, topping the pan up with water if the ginger beer doesn't cover the top of the gammon. Bring the pan up to the boil, cover and transfer to the preheated oven for about 1 hour 40 minutes (20 minutes per 500g/1 lb 2 oz plus 20 minutes over).

Remove the gammon from the oven and leave to cool in the pan until just warm.

Increase the oven temperature to 220°C/Fan 200°C/Gas 7 and line a small roasting tin with foil.

Remove the skin from the ham while still warm so you are left with only a thin layer of fat. Score the fat using a sharp knife.

Mix the ginger bulbs, ground ginger and 3 tablespoons of the ginger syrup from the stem ginger jar in a small bowl. Spread over the top of the gammon.

Put the gammon into the prepared tin and pull up the sides of the foil to cover the lean end of the gammon.

Roast in the preheated oven for 15–20 minutes until golden brown on top.

Bulgar wheat salad with feta, mint and pomegranate

SERVES 4 – 6

225g (8 oz) bulgar wheat

4 spring onions, sliced

a small bunch of fresh parsley,
    chopped

a small bunch of fresh mint,
    chopped

150g (5½ oz) pomegranate seeds

200g (7 oz) feta cheese, crumbled

Dressing

1½ tbsp Dijon mustard

2 tbsp white wine vinegar

4 tbsp olive oil

1 tbsp caster sugar

To prepare ahead
The salad can be assembled
up to 8 hours ahead – dress
up to an hour before serving.
Not suitable for freezing.

This recipe was devised by Luc (photo on left), who has worked by my side for 21 years. It is one of our favourite salads and has a wonderful bright colour, too.

Measure the bulgar wheat into a bowl. Pour over just enough boiling water to cover. Cover the bowl tightly with cling film and set aside for about 30 minutes until the liquid has been absorbed completely. Stir with a fork to fluff up. Set aside to cool.

Add all the salad ingredients to the cold bulgar wheat, season with salt and pepper and stir to mix.

Measure all the dressing ingredients into a bowl, whisk by hand and pour over the salad just before serving.

Roasted fennel and lentil salad

2 bulbs fennel, core removed and chopped into large pieces

2 red peppers, deseeded and chopped into large pieces

2 tbsp olive oil

1 x 85g packet lamb's lettuce

2 heads red chicory, roughly chopped

2 heads green chicory, roughly chopped

1 x 250g packet ready-to-eat cooked puy lentils

a bunch of fresh basil, roughly chopped

200g (7 oz) feta cheese, crumbled

Pesto dressing

2 tbsp white wine vinegar

4 tbsp olive oil

2 tsp caster sugar

1½ tbsp pesto

To prepare ahead
The salad can be assembled up to 4 hours ahead and dressed just before serving.

To cook in the Aga
Roast the vegetables on the floor of the roasting oven for about 25 minutes.

An interesting salad but one with lots of flavour. If you can't get packets of ready-to-eat lentils use a can, drained and rinsed.

Preheat the oven to 220°C/Fan 200°C/Gas 7.

Scatter the chopped fennel and peppers into the base of a roasting tin. Drizzle over the oil and season with salt and pepper.

Roast in the preheated oven for about 25 minutes until tinged brown and tender. Set aside to cool.

Put the lamb's lettuce and chicory in a large salad bowl. Sprinkle over the lentils, basil and feta cheese. Add the cold vegetables and season with salt and pepper.

Measure all the dressing ingredients into a bowl and whisk until smooth. Pour over the salad and toss just before serving.

Cold desserts

Elderflower fruit salad

½ cantaloupe melon

1 small pineapple

1 large ripe mango

225g (8 oz) black grapes

150ml (¼ pint) elderflower
cordial

To prepare ahead
Can be made up to 6 hours
ahead. Not suitable for
freezing.

You can use lots of different kinds of fruit for this recipe but make sure they are ripe and in season and not ones like peaches, nectarines, apples or pears, as they discolour soon after they are prepared and therefore have to be added at the last moment. You can easily buy elderflower cordial from supermarkets and delis.

Remove the seeds from the melon and slice in half. Remove the skin using a sharp knife. Slice each quarter in half widthways and then cut into thin slices.

Slice the top and bottom off the pineapple. Slice off the skin and remove the core. Cut the flesh into quarters and then into 2cm (¾ in) cubes.

Peel the mango, slice either side of the flat centre stone and cut the flesh into slices.

Cut the grapes in half.

Mix all the prepared fruits in a bowl. Spoon over the cordial and leave to marinate for a minimum of 3 hours before serving – the natural juices from the fruits dilute the cordial to give the perfect syrup.

Madeira-soaked apricots

SERVES 4–6

150g (5½ oz) dried ready-to-eat
    apricots

50g (2 oz) caster sugar

200ml (⅓ pint) water

150ml (¼ pint) Madeira

To prepare ahead
Can be made up to a week
ahead and kept in the fridge.
Not suitable for freezing.

To cook in the Aga
Dissolve the sugar on the
simmering plate, cover and
transfer to the simmering
oven for about 15 minutes.

*The apricots will only serve 4 if accompanied by cream, crème
fraîche or Greek yoghurt but you can make them go further
by serving them with ice cream –* try Mascarpone orange ice
cream *(see page 193).*

Cut the apricots into quarters and transfer to a saucepan. Add the
sugar, water and Madeira and heat gently, stirring until the sugar has
dissolved. Cover and simmer over a low heat for about 15 minutes.

Leave to cool and then transfer to the fridge until needed.

Brandied nectarines

SERVES 6

75g (3 oz) light muscovado sugar

175ml (6 fl oz) water

6 ripe nectarines

4 tbsp brandy

To prepare ahead
Can be made up to 2
hours ahead. Not suitable
for freezing.

These are best made on the day because the cut nectarines will discolour after a few hours. If raspberries are in season add a few just before serving.

Measure the sugar and water into a saucepan, heat gently and stir until the sugar is dissolved.

Cut the nectarines in half and remove the stones. Slice each nectarine into 6 pieces.

Add the brandy and nectarines to the sugar syrup and bring to the boil. Boil for a couple of minutes.

Remove from the heat and set aside to cool.

Serve chilled or at room temperature. They are very good on their own served with ice cream or cream, or served alongside *Lemon panna cotta* (see opposite).

Lemon panna cotta

SERVES 8

3 tbsp water

1 packet (11g) powdered gelatine

600ml (1 pint) double cream

300ml (½ pint) milk

pared rind of 2 large lemons

75g (3 oz) caster sugar

To prepare ahead
Can be made up to 2 days ahead. Can be turned out up to 4 hours ahead and kept in the fridge. Not suitable for freezing.

To cook in the Aga
Sit the cream on the back of the Aga to infuse.

The secret of panna cotta is for it to be set to a jelly with a wobble, rather than one that you could plaster a wall with! Literally translated, panna cotta means cooked cream. This is delicious served with a sharp raw fruit or fruit compote. If you prefer to make vanilla flavoured puddings, replace the lemon rind with 1 teaspoon vanilla extract. This quantity will also fill a 1.2 litre (2 pint) pudding basin, which can then be turned out. Or you could serve it in pretty glasses and decorate it with raspberries.

Lightly oil eight small metal pudding basins or ramekins and turn upside down on kitchen paper to allow the excess oil to drain out.

Measure the cold water into a cup and sprinkle in the gelatine evenly. Set aside to sponge.

Measure the cream, milk, lemon rind and sugar into a pan, and stir gently over a low heat until the sugar has dissolved and the cream has reached scalding point (so you can dip your finger in). Remove from the heat, cover with a lid and set aside to infuse for about 15 minutes.

Strain the cream through a sieve and discard the lemon rind. Add the sponged gelatine to the hot cream and whisk by hand until the gelatine has dissolved (the liquid should still be hot enough to melt the gelatine).

Pour into the prepared pudding basins, cover with cling film and carefully transfer to the fridge to set for a minimum of 6 hours or ideally overnight.

To serve, briefly dip each mould into very hot water and using your finger gently pull the set cream away from the sides of the mould and turn out on to a plate.

Serve with *Brandied nectarines* (see opposite) or *Madeira-soaked apricots* (see page 187).

Meringues with passion fruit and raspberries

SERVES 8

3 large egg whites

175g (6 oz) caster sugar

150ml (¼ pint) double cream

150g (5½ oz) Greek yoghurt

6–8 fresh passion fruit

finely grated zest of 1 large orange

24 fresh raspberries

To prepare ahead
Meringues will stay wrapped in a cool place for up to 2 months or in the freezer for up to 6 months.

To cook in the Aga
Bake the meringues in the simmering oven for about 2 hours.

Meringues are great to have in the cupboard in a plastic bag ready to serve to unexpected guests. In the summer when home-grown fruits are ready to pick, you could use those fruits, if preferred.

Preheat the oven to 140°C/Fan 120°C/Gas 2. Line two large baking sheets with non-stick paper.

Place the egg whites in a large clean bowl and whisk on high speed with an electric mixer until stiff. Gradually add the sugar a teaspoon at a time, still whisking on high speed until all the sugar has incorporated and the meringue is stiff and glossy (this could take up to 8 minutes).

Using a teaspoon, spoon the mixture into 8 rounds – 4 on each baking sheet. Using the back of a spoon smooth the sides and make a shallow well in the centre to create a nest.

Bake in the preheated oven for 1¼–1½ hours, or until the meringue comes off the paper easily and is sealed on top. Turn off the oven and leave the meringues to cool in the oven.

Whisk the cream to soft peaks and fold in the yoghurt.

Cut the passion fruit in half. Scoop out the seeds and pulp of 2 of the passion fruit and stir into the cream. Add the orange zest and stir.

Divide the cream between the cold meringue nests and spoon the pulp from the remaining passion fruit over the cream. Decorate with 3 raspberries on each meringue.

Early pink rhubarb brûlée

SERVES 6

400g (14 oz) early rhubarb, sliced
into 4cm (1½ in) pieces

finely grated zest and juice of 1
clementine or half an orange

50g (2 oz) caster sugar

150ml (¼ pint) double cream

150ml (¼ pint) natural yoghurt

3 tbsp light muscovado sugar

To prepare ahead
Can be made up to 2 days
ahead and kept in the
fridge – sprinkling over the
muscovado sugar 2 hours
before serving. Not suitable
for freezing.

To cook in the Aga
Cook the rhubarb, covered, in
the simmering oven for about
15 minutes until tender.

*It is always very exciting when the first early rhubarb appears,
usually from Yorkshire but maybe the first of your own
home-grown rhubarb. Try this, too, with a mixture of ripe
nectarines and raspberries, sprinkled with a little icing sugar.*

Put the sliced rhubarb, zest and juice into a saucepan and pour over the
caster sugar. Stir over a low heat until the sugar has dissolved. Cover
with a lid and simmer very, very gently, avoiding breaking up the fruit,
for a few minutes until tender. Do not overcook otherwise the rhubarb
will break up.

Divide the rhubarb between 6 Martini glasses or ramekins and set aside
to cool.

Whip the cream to soft peaks and stir in the yoghurt. Divide equally
between the ramekins and smooth the tops.

Sprinkle each one with muscovado sugar and transfer to the fridge for
about 2 hours to give the sugar time to dissolve – it should become like
a runny brûlée topping.

Mascarpone orange ice cream

SERVES 6

4 large eggs, separated

100g (4 oz) caster sugar

1 x 250g tub mascarpone, at room temperature

150ml (¼ pint) double cream, lightly whipped

4 tbsp Cointreau

finely grated zest of 2 oranges

segments of 4 oranges

To prepare ahead
Freezes for up to 3 months.

A very grown-up ice cream with Cointreau, this is exceedingly easy and foolproof. If you haven't any Cointreau, use another orange liqueur or brandy.

Measure the egg whites into a large clean bowl and whisk with an electric hand whisk until stiff. Add the caster sugar a teaspoon at a time, still whisking on maximum speed, until stiff and shiny.

Spoon the mascarpone into a mixing bowl and beat with a wooden spoon until soft. Fold in the double cream, Cointreau and orange zest. Stir in the egg yolks and mix until smooth. Carefully fold in the egg whites.

Spoon into a plastic container and freeze for a minimum of 12 hours.

Segment the oranges or, if you are in a hurry, just peel and slice them.

Serve scoopfuls of the ice cream with a few orange segments and more Cointreau, if liked.

Plum ice cream with syrupy plum compote

SERVES 8

2kg (4 lb 8 oz) Victoria plums

550g (1 lb 4 oz) caster sugar

300ml (½ pint) double cream

4 large eggs, separated

To prepare ahead
Can be made up to a month ahead and both can be frozen. The compote will keep in the fridge for up to 10 days.

This is so delicious and is impressive enough to serve for any occasion. The perfect recipe for using plums from the freezer.

First cut the plums in half and remove the stones.

Measure the plums and 450g of the caster sugar into a large saucepan with 1 tablespoon of water. Stir over a high heat for a couple of minutes, cover, lower the temperature and simmer for about 20 minutes, or until tender, watching that they do not break up. Leave to cool.

Measure 350g (12 oz) of the cooled plums (without syrup) into a food processor and whiz until smooth.

Whisk the cream until soft peaks form and then fold in the plum purée.

Whisk the egg whites with an electric hand whisk until stiff and then add the remaining caster sugar a teaspoon at a time until they are shiny and very stiff. Fold in the egg yolks and then the cream and plum mixture.

Spoon into a large plastic container and freeze for at least 8 hours.

Scoop the ice cream into balls and serve with the remaining syrupy plums.

Chocolate meringue torte

SERVES 6 - 8

3 large eggs, separated

175g (6 oz) caster sugar

Chocolate filling

150ml (¼ pint) milk

50g (2 oz) caster sugar

1 x 200g bar plain Bourneville chocolate

1 level tbsp cornflour

150ml (¼ pint) double cream

To prepare ahead
The meringues can be made up to 2 months ahead. The chocolate mixture can be made up to a day ahead. Assemble up to 6 hours ahead. Freezes well.

To cook in the Aga
Cook the meringues in the simmering oven for about 1½–2 hours, or until they easily come off the baking sheet.

This looks impressive and is perfect for a special occasion.

Preheat the oven to 140°C/Fan 120°C/Gas 2. Line two baking sheets with non-stick baking paper and draw on 2 x 20cm (8 in) round circles.

Whisk the egg whites in a large clean bowl or mixer on maximum speed until stiff. Gradually add 175g (6 oz) caster sugar a teaspoon at a time until stiff and glossy.

Spread the meringue out on to the circles to make 2 thick rounds. Transfer to the preheated oven for about an hour, or until a pale cream colour and firm to the touch. Switch the oven off and leave to cool in the oven for 2 hours.

To make the filling, heat the milk in a saucepan until nearly boiling. Remove from the heat, add 50g (2 oz) caster sugar and half the chocolate – stir until the chocolate has melted in the hot milk.

Add the cornflour to the egg yolks in a medium bowl and mix together. Pour the hot chocolate milk over the yolks and whisk immediately until combined. Pour back into the saucepan and stir over a low heat until the custard is thick and smooth – this will take about 5 minutes. Be careful not to boil otherwise it will curdle. Set aside to cool.

Whisk the cream until stiff, add the cold chocolate custard and fold together. Whisk again using an electric mixer until thick.

To assemble the torte, sit one disc of meringue on a plate. Spread with half the chocolate mixture and sit the other meringue disc on top. Spread the remaining chocolate mixture on top.

Melt the remaining chocolate in a bowl over a pan of gently simmering water. Using a teaspoon, drizzle the melted chocolate over the torte in zigzag patterns. Chill for an hour to soften the meringue slightly.

Cut into wedges and serve from the fridge.

Wicked chocolate mousse

SERVES 6 – 8

225g (8 oz) plain chocolate,
    broken into small pieces

a knob of butter

1 tbsp brandy, optional

3 large eggs, separated

150ml (¼ pint) double cream,
    lightly whipped

To prepare ahead
Can be made up to a day
ahead. Freezes well for up to
a month.

To cook in the Aga
Sit the chocolate on the back
of the Aga to melt gently.

---

*Plain and simple chocolate mousse – no frills. A good
pudding to serve if you have all ages coming for lunch.
It can be made in glasses or ramekins.*

Measure the chocolate into a bowl and sit over a saucepan of
simmering water. Melt slowly and do not allow the chocolate to become
too hot.

Stir in the butter, brandy and egg yolks one at a time and mix until
combined. Set aside to cool a little.

Whip the egg whites until just stiff. Fold into the chocolate mixture
with the whipped cream. Fold to combine.

Spoon into a glass bowl (1 litre/1¾ pint capacity) or 6 stemmed glasses
or ramekins. Transfer to the fridge to set.

Serve with fresh summer berries or a winter compote of oranges.

Lemon soufflé mousse

SERVES 6

4 large eggs, separated

100g (4 oz) caster sugar

3 tbsp cold water

1 packet (11g) powdered gelatine

zest and juice of 2 large lemons

To prepare ahead
Can be made up to a day
ahead and kept in the fridge.
Not suitable for freezing.

To cook in the Aga
Sit the sponged gelatine
on the back of the Aga to
dissolve.

The lightest of mousses as there is no cream added – a perfect ending to a special lunch.

You will need a 1.2 litre (2 pint) pretty glass bowl.

Place the egg whites in a large clean bowl and whisk with an electric mixer until stiff.

Place the egg yolks and sugar in a mixing bowl and whisk with an electric hand whisk until light, fluffy and creamy (this will take about 4–5 minutes).

Measure the cold water into a small bowl, sprinkle over the gelatine and set aside to sponge for about 5 minutes until all the water is absorbed. Place the bowl in a pan of simmering water and slowly warm until the gelatine has dissolved and is a clear liquid. Remove from the pan and leave to cool a little.

Stir the lemon zest and juice into the egg yolk mixture. Pour in the dissolved gelatine and mix until smooth.

Spoon four large tablespoons of the whisked egg whites into the lemon mixture and mix until smooth. Carefully fold in the remaining egg whites until they are all combined.

Spoon into the glass dish and transfer to the fridge to set for a minimum of 4 hours.

Serve with some pouring cream and fresh raspberries.

Late summer pudding

SERVES 6 – 8

approx 1.2kg (2 lb 12 oz) mixture of
    British summer soft fruits e.g.
    175g (6 oz) blackcurrants
    175g (6 oz) redcurrants
    225g (8 oz) blackberries
    350g (12 oz) raspberries
    350g (12 oz) strawberries,
        each cut into quarters
225g (8 oz) caster sugar
2–3 tablespoons crème de cassis
    liqueur
3 slices medium sliced bread
    (a day or two old is best),
    crusts removed

To prepare ahead
Can be made up to 2 days
ahead and kept in the fridge.
Freezes well in the basin after
weighting overnight for up to
3 months.

*Choosing different fruits, depending on what is available,
gives this recipe a lovely variation in flavour every time
you prepare it. I try to avoid too many blackcurrants as the
flavour and colour can dominate. Try black cherries or a little
rhubarb for a change. Do not worry if all the fruits do not fit
into the basin, it is nice to serve some extra in a bowl.*

You will need a 1.2 litre (2 pint) pudding basin lined with cling film.

Measure the blackcurrants into a wide saucepan, add the sugar and
cook gently over a low heat, stirring until the sugar has dissolved and
the juices begin to run out. Add the redcurrants and cook for another
couple of minutes.

Stir in the remaining fruit and cassis and cook for a minute. If time
allows, leave the mixture to sit for about 30 minutes so the juices all mix
in (this is not essential).

Cut a round of bread to fit neatly into the base of the prepared pudding
basin and on the top. Cut the remaining slices to fit neatly around the
sides of the basin (do not overlap the bread).

Dip the bread into the fruit mixture, so that it soaks up the juices.
Arrange the red side of the bread touching the basin (this ensures you
have no white patches when the pudding is turned out).

Spoon the fruit and remaining juices into the basin and cover the
surface, loosely, with another piece of bread. Put a side plate or saucer
on top and sit a can or jar on top of this to act as a weight.

Leave the pudding in the fridge to chill for a minimum of 8 hours or
overnight.

To serve, remove the weight and plate and invert the pudding on to a
serving plate. Remove the basin and cling film and serve in wedges with
cream or crème fraîche.

Lemon and lime cheesecakes

SERVES 8

100g (4 oz) Digestive biscuits

50g (2 oz) butter

1 tbsp caster sugar

Filling

1 x 250g tub mascarpone

1 x 375g can full-fat condensed
    milk

juice of 1 small lemon

3 tbsp lemon curd

finely grated zest and juice of 2
    limes

To prepare ahead
Can be made up to 24 hours
ahead – decorating with
raspberries and icing sugar
before serving. Not suitable
for freezing.

*If you don't have cooking rings, you can use small empty
chopped tomato or baked bean cans. Take off the top and
base with a can opener and wash thoroughly. This mixture
can also be made in a 20cm (8 in) shallow springform tin.
Watch out – there is now a low-fat condensed milk available.
If you use this, it won't set!*

Line a baking sheet with cling film and sit 8 x 5cm (2 in) cooking rings
on top.

Crush the biscuits with a rolling pin until they are fine crumbs.

Melt the butter in a pan and add the crumbs and sugar. Stir until
combined. Using a teaspoon, press biscuit crumbs into the base of each
ring to give an even layer. Transfer to the fridge to firm up while making
the filling.

Measure the mascarpone and condensed milk into a bowl and whisk
with an electric hand whisk until smooth.

Add the lemon juice and curd and nearly all the lime zest (reserve some
for garnish) and juice and whisk again until thick and creamy.

Spoon on top of the biscuit base in the rings. Level the tops, cover with
cling film and chill for a minimum of 2 hours.

Decorate with the reserved lime zest and extra fresh raspberries on the
side, if liked.

Boozy red jelly

SERVES 6

1½ packets (16g) powdered
     gelatine

600ml (1 pint) rosé wine

350g (12 oz) caster sugar

450g (1 lb) fresh raspberries

To prepare ahead
Can be made up to 2 days
ahead and kept in the fridge.
Not suitable for freezing.

---

*This is so simple and the combination of rosé and fruits is
wonderful. If you haven't any rosé, use white wine.*

Line a 900g (2 lb) loaf tin with cling film – it will be easier if you wet the
tin first and then the cling film will stick.

Measure 5 tablespoons of cold water into a small bowl. Sprinkle over
the gelatine and leave to sponge for about 5 minutes.

Measure the rosé wine into a saucepan, add the sugar and stir over a
low heat until the sugar is dissolved. Add the sponged gelatine and stir
to dissolve. Remove from the heat and stir in the raspberries.

Pour half of the mixture into the loaf tin (leave the remainder in the
saucepan and keep at room temperature) and chill the loaf tin in the
fridge until set for about an hour.

Once just set, pour the remainder of jelly from the saucepan into the
loaf tin and transfer to the fridge for another 2 hours, or until firm.
(This is done in two batches so that the raspberries are suspended in
the middle of the jelly.)

Turn upside down on to a board, remove the cling film and cut into
thick slices.

Serve with crème fraîche or Greek yoghurt.

Divine brown bread
ice cream

SERVES 6

15g (½ oz) butter

75g (3 oz) fine brown
    breadcrumbs

75g (3 oz) light muscovado sugar

600ml (1 pint) double cream

1 x 375g can full-fat condensed
    milk

To prepare ahead
Can be made up to 2 months
ahead.

*This is a gem of an ice cream – no need for an ice cream
maker, no eggs and no need to whisk half way through
freezing. The brown breadcrumbs are simply caramelised
with sugar in a frying pan.*

Melt the butter in a non-stick frying pan, add the breadcrumbs and
gently toast over a low heat, stirring all the time until lightly golden.

Sprinkle in half the sugar and continue to fry over a high heat until
crispy and golden. Be very careful not to burn them. Tip on to a plate,
toss in the remaining sugar and leave to cool.

Whisk the double cream in a bowl until soft peaks form. Add the
condensed milk and fold together. Whisk again until the mixture
reaches the soft peak stage once more.

Fold in the cold breadcrumbs until well combined.

Pour into a plastic container, cover and freeze for a minimum of 12
hours.

Serve in scoops with fresh fruit or a tart.

Classic lemon tart

SERVES 8

Pastry

225g (8 oz) plain flour

150g (5½ oz) cold butter, cut
   into small cubes

25g (1 oz) icing sugar

1 large egg, beaten

2 tbsp water

Lemon filling

9 large eggs

300ml (½ pint) double cream

350g (12 oz) caster sugar

finely grated zest and juice of 6
   large lemons

To prepare ahead

Can be made up to 2 days
ahead. Freezes well.

To cook in the Aga

Bake the pastry blind on
the grid shelf on the floor
of the roasting oven for 10
minutes. Remove the paper
and beans and cook for a
further 10 minutes. Fill the
tart and slide back on to the
floor with the cold shelf on
the second set of runners for
15 minutes, or until just set
with a slight wobble. Transfer
to the simmering oven for 20
minutes until completely set.

Delicious crisp pastry with a smooth lemon filling. Best served warm or cold.

You will need a 28cm (11 in) deep, loose-bottomed tart tin.

To make the pastry, measure the flour, butter and sugar into a processor. Whiz until the mixture looks like breadcrumbs and then add the egg and water. Whiz again until it forms a ball.

Roll out the pastry very thinly on a floured work surface until it is just a little bigger than the size of the tin. Line the tart tin with the pastry, letting the extra pastry hang over the sides of the tin. Place on a baking sheet and then chill in the fridge for 30 minutes.

Preheat the oven to 200°C/Fan 180°C/Gas 6.

Line the tin with non-stick baking paper and fill with baking beans. Blind bake for 15 minutes in the preheated oven until pale golden brown.

Take out of the oven and remove the baking beans and paper. Carefully trim the excess pastry from the sides using a sharp knife. Return the empty pastry shell to the oven for another 10–12 minutes, or until it is completely dry. Set aside to cool.

Reduce the temperature of the oven to 160°C/Fan 140°C/Gas 3.

Measure all of the filling ingredients into a bowl and whisk until smooth. Carefully pour the filling mixture into the cold baked pastry case.

Transfer the tart and tray carefully to the oven and bake for about 40–45 minutes, or until just set but with a slight wobble in the middle. The filling will sink down a bit when it has cooled.

Leave to cool a little or completely and then remove it from the tin. Transfer to a serving plate and dust with icing sugar to serve.

Hot puddings

Steamed syrup pudding

SERVES 4 – 6

5 tbsp golden syrup

100g (4 oz) soft butter

100g (4 oz) caster sugar

100g (4 oz) self-raising flour

1 level tsp baking powder

2 large eggs

2 tbsp milk

To prepare ahead
Can be made up to a day
ahead and gently reheated,
still in the pudding basin, on
the hob in hot water. Freezes
well cooked for up to 3
months.

To cook in the Aga
Sit the basin in a large pan
and bring to the boil on
the boiling plate, cover and
transfer to the simmering
oven for about 1½ hours.

---

*Most people love the comfort of a nursery-style pudding,
especially in winter. This one is always popular, even with
people who would not normally eat puddings. Use the same
recipe for a jam pudding, replacing the syrup with a red jam
of your choice.*

Generously butter an 850ml or 1.2 litre (1½ or 2 pint) pudding basin
and cut a square of foil to fit neatly into the base.

Measure the ingredients into a bowl and whisk with an electric hand
whisk until blended. Spoon the mixture into the prepared basin and
smooth the surface. (There will be extra space above the mixture if you
use a 1.2 litre [2 pint] basin.)

Cut a generous square of both non-stick baking paper and foil (they
should be large enough to overhang the top) and fold a pleat in the
centre of each (this allows for the sponge to rise). Lay the paper first
and then the foil on top and tightly twist around the edges to seal or
secure with a piece of string.

Sit a metal pastry cutter in the base of a steamer or large saucepan and
lower the basin on to it (this protects the base of the sponge from overcooking). Pour simmering water into the pan until it reaches half way
up the sides of the basin. Cover with a lid and steam over a low heat for
about 1½ hours (keep checking if the water needs topping up).

Remove the paper and foil and turn the pudding out. (Don't forget to
remove the base square of foil if attached to the sponge!)

Serve hot with custard and cream. If you can find an excuse, serve with
extra warm golden syrup, too – just heat some in a pan.

Baked rice pudding

SERVES 6

50g (2 oz) pudding rice

2 level tbsp caster sugar

½ tsp vanilla extract

600ml (1 pint) full-fat milk

a knob of butter

To prepare ahead
Do not make ahead – cook and serve. Not suitable for freezing.

To cook in the Aga
Slide on to the grid shelf on the floor of the roasting oven and cook for about 20 minutes, then carefully transfer to the simmering oven for about 2 hours.

This is a classic recipe and perfect for a Sunday lunch. Lucy's mother suggests that if you are in a hurry, you can put the rice and milk in a saucepan and bring to the boil, stirring so the rice does not stick – this reduces the cooking time by almost half. But on no account make it fluffy in the saucepan on the hob. A thick, short-grained rice (Carolina rice, usually labelled pudding rice) should be used so that the maximum amount of milk can be absorbed. This method, with its long, slow cooking, will give a rich and creamy consistency. You can use a 1.2 litre (2 pint) dish, if you prefer, but the rice will not come to the top.

Preheat the oven to 160°C/Fan 140°C/Gas 3. You will need a 1 litre (1¾ pint) shallow ovenproof dish, well buttered.

Wash the rice well and scatter over the base of the buttered dish.

Measure the sugar and vanilla into a jug and add the milk. Pour this over the rice, stir a touch and dot with the butter.

Transfer to the preheated oven and bake for about 2–2¼ hours, or until golden brown. Stir once or twice with a fork during the first hour, just before the skin forms.

If the pudding is looking quite thick before the grains are tender, heat a little more milk and stir in. A bit like custard, some people like it runny, and some like it thick!

Serve hot or cold with cream and home-made summer fruit jam.

Quick orange and plum crumble

SERVES 6

900g (2 lb) fresh plums, halved and stoned

finely grated rind of 1 orange

1 tbsp orange juice

175g (6 oz) granulated sugar

Crumble

175g (6 oz) plain flour

75g (3 oz) butter, cubed

50g (2 oz) Demerara sugar

To prepare ahead
Both parts can be made up to a day ahead and assembled up to 4 hours ahead. Freezes well assembled but uncooked.

To cook in the Aga
Bake on the second set of runners in the roasting oven for about 35 minutes.

You can use frozen plums, if preferred – in which case defrost the plums until you can just cut them in half. Remove the stone, tip the plums into a bowl, add the sugar and orange rind and juice and continue. If you leave them to completely defrost they will lose their colour. You need to cook the crumble a bit longer because it will take a little longer to brown.

Preheat the oven to 200°C/Fan 180°C/Gas 6. You will need a 1.7–2 litre (3–3½ pint) shallow ovenproof dish.

Put the raw plums, orange rind and juice and granulated sugar in the dish and toss together.

Measure the flour and butter into a processor and whiz until it looks like breadcrumbs. Tip into a bowl, stir in the Demerara sugar and sprinkle on top of the plums. Level the top.

Bake in the preheated oven for about 30–40 minutes, or until pale golden brown on top and bubbling around the edges.

Variations

Apple Crumble
900g (2 lb) Bramley apples, peeled weight (windfalls will do)

Apple and Mulberry or Blackberry
600g (1 lb 5 oz) Bramley apples, peeled weight, and 300g (10 oz) mulberries or blackberries (use two thirds apple and one third mulberries or blackberries)

Sticky toffee pudding with ginger

This is lovely and rich and just right for a special occasion – leave the ginger out if it is not your thing. This will make a generous amount of sauce, which is very useful for serving separately.

SERVES 6 – 8

Pudding

75g (3 oz) soft butter

150g (5½ oz) light muscovado sugar

2 large eggs

175g (6 oz) self-raising flour

1 tsp bicarbonate of soda

2 tbsp black treacle

1 tsp vanilla extract

125ml (4 fl oz) milk

5 bulbs of stem ginger in syrup, drained and finely chopped

Sauce

110g (4½ oz) soft butter

250g (9 oz) light muscovado sugar

400ml (14 fl oz) double cream

½ tsp vanilla extract

Preheat the oven to 180°C/Fan 160°C/Gas 4 and lightly grease a 2 litre (3½ pint) shallow ovenproof dish.

First make the pudding – measure the soft butter and sugar into a mixing bowl. Whisk using an electric hand whisk until light and creamy. Add the other ingredients and whisk again until a smooth, thick batter forms.

Pour into the prepared dish and bake in the preheated oven for about 50–55 minutes until well risen and coming away from the sides of the dish and springy to the touch.

To make the sauce, measure all the ingredients into a saucepan. Gently heat until the butter has melted and then boil for a couple of minutes, stirring all the time.

Pour half the sauce over the pudding in its dish and serve warm with extra sauce and cream.

To prepare ahead
The pudding can be made up to a day ahead and reheated gently in a low oven. The sauce can be made up to 3 days ahead. Both freeze well.

To cook in the Aga
Bake on the grid shelf on the floor of the roasting oven with the cold sheet on the second set of runners for about 45 minutes.

Magical lemon soufflé pudding

SERVES 6

50g (2 oz) softened butter

225g (8 oz) caster sugar

50g (2 oz) self-raising flour

3 large eggs, separated

450ml (16 fl oz) milk

juice and finely grated rind of
   2 large lemons

> **To prepare ahead**
> Can be made in the morning
> and reheated for about 30
> minutes in a low oven 140°C/
> Fan120°C/Gas 2 or in the
> simmering oven of the Aga.
> Not suitable for freezing.
>
> **To cook in the Aga**
> Bake on the grid shelf on the
> floor of the roasting oven
> with the cold sheet on the
> second set of runners for
> about 45 minutes.

This is that wonderful pudding with a soufflé top and a sharp lemon sauce underneath. A perfect pudding to make from store cupboard ingredients and a couple of lemons. To make individual puds use about ten size 1 soufflé dishes filled almost to the top and cook them at the same temperature for about 30 minutes.

Preheat the oven to 180°C/Fan160°C/Gas 4 and butter a 1.4–1.7 litre (2½–3 pint) wide-based, ovenproof dish.

Measure the butter, sugar, flour and egg yolks into a processor and whiz until smooth.

Pour the milk, lemon juice and rind through the funnel and whiz again until mixed. It may look curdled at this stage – don't worry!

Whisk the egg whites in a large bowl until stiff.

Pour the lemon mixture into the bowl with the egg whites and use the whisk to stir gently until combined. Tip into the buttered dish.

Stand the dish in a roasting tin and pour boiling water around the dish to come halfway up the side. Carefully transfer to the preheated oven for about 50 minutes until pale golden and set.

Serve and you will see the sponge on top and the lemon sauce underneath.

Blackberry soufflé

SERVES 6-8

300g (10 oz) fresh or frozen
  blackberries

1 heaped tbsp cornflour

3 tbsp crème de cassis

3 large egg whites

100g (4 oz) caster sugar

icing sugar, to serve

To prepare ahead
Can be made up to 5 hours
ahead – keep in the fridge
and then cook a little longer
to serve. Not suitable for
freezing.

To cook in the Aga
Bake in a bain-marie on the
grid shelf on the floor of
the roasting oven for 8–10
minutes until well risen.

*This really is the most simple soufflé to make and it is just
wonderful to eat. The quantities will serve 6–8, depending on
which size of ramekin you choose.If you haven't any crème de
cassis, use kirsch or leave it out.*

Preheat the oven to 190°C/Fan170°C/Gas 5 and place a baking sheet
in the oven to get hot. Grease the insides of 8 size 1 ramekins or 6 large
ramekins.

Put the blackberries into a saucepan. Gently heat for 4–5 minutes until
the fruits are soft and mushy.

Mix the cornflour and crème de cassis together until smooth.

Pour a little of the blackberry mixture on to the cornflour and cassis,
blend well and then add to the blackberries in the pan. Stir over the
heat until thickened.

Sieve the mixture into a bowl and then leave to become cold.

Whisk the egg whites until stiff. Add the sugar a teaspoon at a time until
the mixture is stiff and shiny.

Fold the cold blackberry purée into the egg whites and carefully mix
until combined and smooth. Spoon into the ramekins and level the
tops. Run your finger around the top edge of the ramekin dish to make
the sides even – this will give an even rise.

Place the ramekins on the hot baking sheet and cook in the preheated
oven for 8 minutes until well risen.

Dust with icing sugar and serve at once.

Apple, almond and honey dessert cake

SERVES 8

350g (12 oz) self-raising flour

225g (8 oz) caster sugar

4 tbsp honey

3 large eggs

1 tsp almond extract

225g (8 oz) butter, melted

450g (1 lb) cooking apples, peeled
 and cored

50g (2 oz) flaked almonds

icing sugar, to serve

To prepare ahead
Can be made up to 2 days
ahead and reheated in a low
oven to serve. Freezes well
cooked for up to 3 months.

To cook in the Aga
Slide on to the grid shelf
on the floor of the roasting
oven with the cold sheet on
the second set of runners for
about 20 minutes or until
pale golden brown. Transfer
the now hot cold sheet to
the middle of the simmering
oven and sit the cake on top
and bake for a further hour,
or until a skewer comes out
clean when inserted into the
centre of the cake.

---

*This is a wonderful open cake full of flavour and is perfect for
using up windfall apples in season. Best served warm with a
generous amount of cream.*

Preheat the oven to 140°C/Fan 120°C/Gas 2. You will need a 28 x 4cm
(11 x 1½ in) loose-bottomed tart tin, really well greased.

Measure the flour, sugar, honey, eggs, almond extract and melted butter
into a mixing bowl. Beat with a wooden spoon or electric mixer until
combined and smooth.

Spread half this mixture over the base of the tart tin. Thickly slice
the apples and lay them on top of the mixture. Spoon the remaining
mixture on top of the apples so they are completely covered in an even
layer. Sprinkle over the flaked almonds.

Bake in the centre of the preheated oven for about 1¼ hours, or until
golden brown and the sponge is cooked.

Dust with icing sugar and serve warm with cream.

Higgledy piggledy pie

SERVES 6 – 8

900g (2 lb) Bramley apples,
    peeled and thickly sliced

450g (1 lb) fresh or frozen
    blackberries

175g (6 oz) caster sugar

5 level tbsp cornflour

Pastry

175g (6 oz) plain flour

2 level tbsp icing sugar

100g (4 oz) cold butter

1 large egg, beaten

a little milk and Demerara sugar
    to glaze

To prepare ahead
Can be made a day ahead and
reheated in a hot oven for
about 15 minutes. Freezes well
cooked or uncooked for up to
3 months.

To cook in the Aga
Bake on the second set of
runners in the roasting oven
for about 30–35 minutes.

An apple and blackberry pie with a difference. Made in an open, shallow dish, the rough pastry topping rests on the fruit and makes them look like little mounds.

Preheat the oven to 200°C/Fan 180°C/Gas 6. You will need a 28cm (11 in) open, shallow ovenproof dish.

Measure the apples, blackberries, sugar and cornflour into a bowl and mix together until all the fruit is coated in the cornflour and sugar. Spoon into the dish.

To make the pastry, measure the flour, icing sugar and butter into a processor and whiz until it looks like breadcrumbs. Add the egg and whiz again until a ball is formed.

Roll the pastry on a floured work surface into a circle a few centimetres bigger than the dish you are using. Sit the pastry loosely on top of the fruits so it moulds itself over the top. Brush with a little milk and sprinkle with Demerara sugar.

Bake in the preheated oven for 35–45 minutes, or until golden and bubbling around the edges.

Serve hot with cream.

Apple pie

This is a classic – an all-time favourite with all ages for Sunday lunch.

SERVES 6

25g (1 oz) butter

1kg (2.2 lb) Bramley apples, peeled, cored and thickly sliced

100g (4 oz) Demerara sugar

½ tsp cinnamon

Pastry

175g (6 oz) plain flour

100g (4 oz) cold butter

25g (1 oz) caster sugar

about 3 tbsp water

a little milk and sugar, for glazing

To prepare ahead

Can be made up to a day ahead and reheated in a moderate oven for about 15 minutes. Freezes well cooked for up to 3 months.

To cook in the Aga

Cook on the second set of runners in the roasting oven for about 35 minutes. If getting too brown slide the cold sheet above.

You will need a 1.2 litre (2 pint) pie dish with a lip and a pie funnel or a small dish to place inside.

Melt the butter in a saucepan over a high heat and add the apples and sugar. Toss over the heat until the sugar has dissolved and the apples are just starting to soften. Sprinkle in the cinnamon and spoon into the pie dish around the funnel or small dish.

To make the pastry, measure the flour and butter into a processor and whiz until it looks like breadcrumbs. Add the sugar and water and whiz again to form a ball.

Roll the pastry out on a floured work surface until it is 4cm (1½ in) bigger than the pie dish. Brush the edge of the dish with water. Cut a thin 1cm (½ in) strip from the edge of the pastry and lay on the edges of the dish and press down. Brush the strip with water. Lay the rest of the pastry over the top of the dish, pressing down on to the pastry strip to seal. Trim and flute the edges and then chill for 30 minutes.

Preheat the oven to 200°C/Fan 180°C/Gas 6.

Glaze the pie with a little milk and then sprinkle with sugar before baking in the preheated oven for about 35 minutes, or until the pastry is pale golden and the apples are cooked through. If the edges of the pastry are getting too brown cover loosely with a piece of foil.

Serve hot with *Real pouring custard* (see page 222) and cream.

Blackcurrant pie

SERVES 6

Pastry

225g (8 oz) plain flour

150g (5½ oz) butter

25g (1 oz) icing sugar

1 large egg

a little milk and Demerara sugar,
    to glaze

Filling

500g (1 lb 2 oz) blackcurrants

75g (3 oz) caster sugar

2 level tbsp cornflour

To prepare ahead
Can be made up to a day
ahead and reheated in a
preheated oven 160°C/Fan
140°C/Gas 3 for about 15
minutes. Freezes well cooked
or uncooked for up to 3
months.

To cook in the Aga
Bake on the grid shelf on
the floor of the roasting
oven for about 20 minutes,
then remove the grid shelf
and bake on the floor of the
roasting oven for 10 minutes,
or until golden.

*This is one of our favourites at the moment, using
blackcurrants from the garden. If you don't have an
oblong flan tin, use a 20cm (8 in) round flan tin.*

Preheat the oven to 220°C/Fan 200°C/Gas 7. You will need an oblong
flan tin about 35 x 13cm (14 x 5 in).

To make the pastry, measure the flour and butter into a processor and
whiz until it looks like breadcrumbs. Add the sugar and egg and whiz
again to form a ball.

Roll two thirds of the pastry out on a floured work surface into an
oblong and line the flan tin.

Measure the blackcurrants, sugar and cornflour into a bowl and mix to
combine. Spoon into the pastry-lined tin.

Roll out the remaining pastry and lay over the fruit, pressing down on
to the edges of the tin. Trim and seal the edges. Brush with a little milk
and sprinkle with Demerara sugar to glaze.

Bake in the preheated oven for about 30–35 minutes, or until golden
and bubbling.

Serve hot with cream.

Apricot bread and butter pudding

SERVES 6

100g (4 oz) sultanas

2 tbsp Cointreau, Grand Marnier or brandy

4 tbsp apricot jam

8 medium slices of white bread, generously buttered on one side

3 large eggs

300ml (½ pint) milk

150ml (5 fl oz) double cream

½ tsp vanilla extract

50g (2 oz) caster sugar

25g (1 oz) Demerara sugar

To prepare ahead
The sandwiches can be made, lined in the dish, covered in cling film and chilled up to a day ahead. The custard can also be made a day ahead. Pour the custard over the sandwiches up to an hour before cooking as detailed (right). Not suitable for freezing.

To cook in the Aga
Bake on the second set of runners in the roasting oven for about 25 minutes.

This pudding also works well made with marmalade – substitute four tablespoons of marmalade for the apricot jam.

Preheat the oven to 200°C/Fan 180°C/Gas 6. You will need a 1.7 litre (3 pint) shallow ovenproof dish, buttered.

Measure the sultanas into a bowl and pour over the liqueur. Leave to soak in a warm place for about an hour.

Spread the jam on 4 of the slices of bread and sit the remaining slices on top to give you 4 apricot sandwiches. Trim off the crusts and discard. Cut each sandwich into four triangles.

Arrange the triangles in the buttered dish so the points are sticking up. Scatter the soaked sultanas over the top (and any extra liqueur in the bowl).

Measure the eggs, milk, cream, vanilla and caster sugar into a jug and whisk by hand until combined. Pour the custard over the bread.

Sprinkle with Demerara sugar and, if time allows, set aside for 30–60 minutes for the bread to absorb the liquid.

Bake in the preheated oven for about 25–30 minutes until golden brown and puffed up.

Sprinkle with icing sugar and serve straight away, with extra cream if liked.

Wicked chocolate squares with ganache sauce

MAKES 30 SQUARES

300g (10 oz) butter, cubed

300g (10 oz) Bourneville chocolate, broken into pieces

300g (10 oz) light muscovado sugar

4 large eggs

100g (4 oz) self-raising flour

Ganache sauce

150g (5½ oz) Bourneville chocolate, broken into pieces

200ml (⅓ pint) pouring double cream

To prepare ahead
Can be made up to a day ahead and warmed through in a low oven. Sauce can be made up to 2 days ahead and gently reheated on the hob. Both freeze well cooked for up to 3 months.

To cook in the Aga
Bake on the grid shelf on the floor of the roasting oven with the cold sheet on the second set of runners for about 20 minutes. Transfer the hot cold sheet into the simmering oven and sit the cake on top and bake for a further 20 minutes.

These are simply to die for. Always a favourite on restaurant menus.

Preheat the oven to 190°C/Fan 170°C/Gas 5. Grease and line a traybake tin or a small roasting tin about 30 x 23cm (12 x 9 in) with foil.

Measure the butter and chocolate into a bowl. Place over a pan of simmering water and gently melt together until smooth. Set aside.

Whisk together the sugar and eggs until blended. Pour in the melted butter and chocolate mixture and stir until smooth. Sieve in the flour and mix well. Pour into the lined tin.

Bake in the preheated oven for 40–45 minutes until a light crust has formed on the top and the middle is set.

Meanwhile, to make the ganache sauce, measure the chocolate and cream into a bowl and sit over a pan of gently simmering water and stir until melted.

Cut the cake into squares and pour the ganache sauce over the top to serve.

Real pouring custard

SERVES 6

2 large eggs, plus 1 large egg yolk

1 heaped tsp cornflour

25g (1 oz) caster sugar

1–2 tsp vanilla extract

300ml (½ pint) full-fat milk

300ml (½ pint) double cream

To prepare ahead
Can be made up to 2 days ahead. Not suitable for freezing.

No Sunday lunch is complete without a delicious pudding and real custard. This is rich and creamy – you can make it with semi-skimmed milk, if that's what you have in the fridge, but it will be slightly less rich.

Measure the eggs, yolk, cornflour, sugar and vanilla into a mixing bowl and, using a hand balloon whisk, blend to combine.

Measure the milk and cream into a saucepan and gently warm over a simmering heat. Pour on to the egg mixture in the bowl and immediately whisk again until smooth and combined.

Rinse the saucepan, strain the custard through a sieve into the saucepan and heat over a low heat. Stir continuously with a wooden spoon until the custard thickens and coats the back of the spoon. Be very careful not to get it too hot otherwise the custard will curdle.

Pour into a jug and cover with cling film until needed. Serve cold or reheat gently in a saucepan to serve.

Aga roasting chart

There are often different methods for roasting in the Aga. Classically, you can roast meat in the roasting oven. However, you can also slow roast for part of the roasting time in the simmering oven. Coarser cuts are better cooked slowly and prime cuts are best roasted at a high temperature. Always rest the meat before carving it to retain the juices and flavour in the meat.

Roast beef

Season the meat and place it in a roasting tin.

Fast roasting for prime cuts of beef (sirloin, rib or topside – for fillet see below)
Hang the tin on the lowest set of runners in the roasting oven and roast for:

On the bone	12 minutes per 450g (1 lb)
Off the bone	15 minutes per 450g (1 lb)

These times give a pink, medium-rare centre – if you like it well done, add 5 minutes per 450g (1 lb).

Slow roasting for less tender cuts (brisket and silverside)
Brown the joint in the roasting oven on both sides (this takes about 30 minutes) and then transfer to the simmering oven, covered with foil, to roast for:

1½ hours per 450g (1 lb)

Fillet of beef (for a 1.8–2.7kg [4–6 lb] fillet)
Brown the meat in a frying pan on the boiling plate, and then roast for:

10 minutes per 450g (1 lb) for medium-rare centre
8 minutes per 450g (1 lb) for rare

Roast lamb

Season the meat and place it in a roasting tin.

Fast roasting
Cook at the top of the roasting oven for:

Rare	15 minutes per 450g (1 lb)
Well done	20 minutes per 450g (1 lb)

Slow roasting
See page 60.

Roast pork

For perfect crackling ensure the fat is scored finely and then rub it with oil and salt. If, at the end of cooking, the crackling is not crisp enough, carefully remove the crackling and sit it on a rack in a roasting tin and return to the top of the roasting oven while the meat is resting. Snip the crackling with scissors and serve alongside the joint.

Season the meat and sit it in a roasting tin.

Fast roasting
Roast at the top of the roasting oven for:

> 25 minutes per 450g (1 lb)

Slow roasting for belly of pork
Pour 1.2 litres (2 pints) water into the roasting tin.

Slow cook in the simmering oven for:

> 5 hours

Transfer to roasting oven to crisp the skin for:

> 30 minutes

Roast turkey

Lightly smear the turkey with butter or oil and season. Fill the cavity with lemon, onion and herbs. Stuff the breast end with a non-meat stuffing. Stand the bird on a grill rack in a roasting tin.

There are two methods of cooking turkey – slow cooking overnight in the simmering oven or short, fast roasting in the roasting oven.

Fast roasting
Baste the bird from time to time during cooking. Cover the breast and legs with foil when golden brown to prevent over-browning.

Slide the roasting tin on to the lowest set of runners in the roasting oven and roast for:

> 3.6–4.5kg (8 lb–10 lb)   about 1¾–2 hours
> 5–7.25kg (11 lb–15 lb 12 oz) about 2–2½ hours
> 7.5–10kg (16 lb 5 oz–22 lb)   about 3 hours

Slow roasting
Wrap the turkey loosely in foil to enclose it and then roast in the simmering oven for:

> 3.6–4.5kg (8 lb–10 lb)   about 8–10 hours
> 5–7.25kg (11 lb–15 lb 12 oz) about 9–12 hours
> 7.5–10kg (16 lb 5 oz–22 lb)   about 10–14 hours

Remove the foil and return to the roasting oven for:

> about 20–40 minutes (according to the size of the bird), or until golden and the skin is crisp

Roast chicken

Lightly smear the chicken with butter or oil and season with salt and pepper. Fill the cavity with lemon, onion and herbs. If the bird gets too brown during cooking, cover the breast with foil.

Stand on a grill rack in a roasting tin and slide on to the lowest set of runners in the roasting oven and roast for:
> 20 minutes per 450g (1 lb)

Roast pheasant

Arrange the birds in a large roasting tin, rub the skin with butter, season with salt and pepper and then lay thin rashers of bacon over the breasts.

Roast in the roasting oven for:
> about 45–50 minutes

Roast partridge

Arrange the birds in a large roasting tin, rub the skin with butter, season with salt and pepper and then lay thin rashers of bacon over the breasts.

Roast in the roasting oven for:
> about 30–35 minutes

Roast duck or goose

Prick the skin all over and sit upside down on a grill rack in a large roasting tin.

Roast on the lowest set of runners in the roasting oven, to allow the bird to brown, for:
> about 30 minutes for goose
> about 20 minutes for duck

Turn over, to brown the breast, and continue to roast for:
> about 20 minutes

Cover loosely with foil and transfer to the simmering oven for:
> about 2 hours for goose
> about 1 hour for duck

Return to the roasting oven to crisp the skin before serving.

Index